The Food Processor Cookbook

Hamlyn Cookshelf Series

The Food Processor

Cookbook

Jill Spencer

Hamlyn

London · New York · Sydney · Toronto

The following titles are also available in this series:

Cooking with Yogurt · Mighty Mince Cookbook
Potato Cookery · Sweets and Candies

The author and publisher would like to thank the
following for their help in sponsoring photographs
for this book:
Carmel Fruit and Vegetables   page 57
ICTC Limited, U.K. distributors of Magimix and
Robot-Chef   pages 46-47 and 76
Knorr   page 19
Mazola Pure Corn Oil   page 48
Olives from Spain   pages 45 and 75
Sharwoods Foods Limited   page 112

Front cover photograph by James Jackson
Photography by John Lee
Line illustrations by The Hayward Art Group

First published in 1979 under the title of
Kitchen Magic with food processors by
The Hamlyn Publishing Group Limited
London · New York · Sydney · Toronto
Astronaut House, Feltham, Middlesex, England

This edition published in 1984
© Copyright The Hamlyn Publishing Group Limited, 1979, 1984

ISBN 0 600 32425 7

Phototypeset by Photocomp Limited, Birmingham, England

Printed in Yugoslavia

Contents

Useful facts and figures

Notes on metrication

In this book quantities are given in metric and Imperial measures. Exact conversion from Imperial to metric measures does not usually give very convenient working quantities and so the metric measures have been rounded off into units of 25 grams. The table below shows the recommended equivalents.

Ounces	Approx. g to nearest whole figure	Recommended conversion to nearest unit of 25	Ounces	Approx. g to nearest whole figure	Recommended conversion to nearest unit of 25
1	28	25	11	312	300
2	57	50	12	340	350
3	85	75	13	368	375
4	113	100	14	396	400
5	142	150	15	425	425
6	170	175	16 (1 lb)	454	450
7	198	200	17	482	475
8	227	225	18	510	500
9	255	250	19	539	550
10	283	275	20 (1¼ lb)	567	575

Note: When converting quantities over 20 oz first add the appropriate figures in the centre column, then adjust to the nearest unit of 25. As a general guide, 1 kg (1000 g) equals 2.2 lb or about 2 lb 3 oz. This method of conversion gives good results in nearly all cases, although in certain pastry and cake recipes a more accurate conversion is necessary to produce a balanced recipe.

Liquid measures The millilitre has been used in this book and the following table gives a few examples.

Imperial	Approx. ml to nearest whole figure	Recommended ml	Imperial	Approx. ml to nearest whole figure	Recommended ml
¼ pint	142	150 ml	1 pint	567	600 ml
½ pint	283	300 ml	1½ pints	851	900 ml
¾ pint	425	450 ml	1¾ pints	992	1000 ml (1 litre)

Spoon measures All spoon measures given in this book are level unless otherwise stated.

Can sizes At present, cans are marked with the exact (usually to the nearest whole number) metric equivalent of the Imperial weight of the contents, so we have followed this practice when giving can sizes.

Oven temperatures

The table below gives recommended equivalents.

	°C	°F	Gas Mark		°C	°F	Gas Mark
Very cool	110	225	$\frac{1}{4}$	Moderately hot	190	375	5
	120	250	$\frac{1}{2}$		200	400	6
Cool	140	275	1	Hot	220	425	7
	150	300	2		230	450	8
Moderate	160	325	3	Very hot	240	475	9
	180	350	4				

Notes for American and Australian users

In America the 8-oz measuring cup is used. In Australia metric measures are now used in conjunction with the standard 250-ml measuring cup. The Imperial pint, used in Britain and Australia, is 20 fl oz, while the American pint is 16 fl oz. It is important to remember that the Australian tablespoon differs from both the British and American tablespoons; the table below gives a comparison. The British standard tablespoon, which has been used throughout this book, holds 17.7 ml, the American 14.2 ml, and the Australian 20 ml. A teaspoon holds approximately 5 ml in all three countries.

British	American	Australian	British	American	Australian
1 teaspoon	1 teaspoon	1 teaspoon	$3\frac{1}{2}$ tablespoons	4 tablespoons	3 tablespoons
1 tablespoon	1 tablespoon	1 tablespoon	4 tablespoons	5 tablespoons	$3\frac{1}{2}$ tablespoons
2 tablespoons	3 tablespoons	2 tablespoons			

An Imperial/American guide to solid and liquid measures

Imperial	American	Imperial	American
Solid measures		**Liquid measures**	
1 lb butter or		$\frac{1}{4}$ pint liquid	$\frac{2}{3}$ cup liquid
margarine	2 cups	$\frac{1}{2}$ pint	$1\frac{1}{4}$ cups
1 lb flour	4 cups	$\frac{3}{4}$ pint	2 cups
1 lb granulated		1 pint	$2\frac{1}{2}$ cups
or castor sugar	2 cups	$1\frac{1}{2}$ pints	$3\frac{3}{4}$ cups
1 lb icing sugar	3 cups	2 pints	5 cups ($2\frac{1}{2}$ pints)
8 oz rice	1 cup		

Note: When making any of the recipes in this book, only follow one set of measures as they are not interchangeable.

Key to symbols

Denotes use of the double-bladed chopping knife

Denotes use of the slicing disc

Denotes use of the grating disc

All about food processors

The food processor must surely be one of the most efficient machines to come on the market in recent years. Whether you are a housewife, have a full-time job and a family to cater for, prepare dishes in bulk for the freezer, or simply enjoy entertaining, the food processor can help you. It takes all the tedious labour and time out of preparing both raw and cooked foods in any recipe.

There are several brands of food processor on the market, each having the same basic design and attachments. They are extremely versatile and can chop, grate, mince, slice, purée, beat or knead, literally in seconds. However they are not designed to aerate mixtures, for example, whisking egg whites.

All the recipes in this book were created using the Magimix (type A) and the Robot-Chef (type B) machines, but they can be easily adapted for other types of food processor, using the manufacturer's instructions as a guide.

The different types of machine are described in a chart, showing the various attachments and their uses (see pages 12–13). **Type A** is supplied as a complete unit with all the attachments. **Type B** is supplied as a complete unit with attachments and is a version of type A. **Type C** has three different units which can be bought separately or as one complete unit. The container is smaller than types A and B, so less food can be mixed or chopped at any one time. **Type D** is similar to type A, and is sold as a complete unit with a double-bladed chopping knife and a reversible disc for slicing and shredding.
A dust cover is available for some machines.

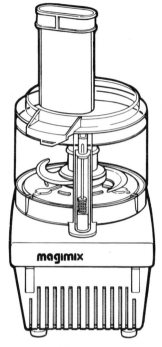

Type A, Magimix

Type B, Robot Chef

How to use your food processor

1 Always read the manufacturer's instructions carefully before use.
2 Never overload the machine, as this will strain the motor. It is far better to prepare small batches of food.
3 The bowl is able to withstand boiling liquid, but this could splash dangerously, so allow liquids to cool before adding them to the bowl.
4 Always let the blades stop moving before removing the lid.
5 Handle the blades carefully as they are sharp, and keep out of the reach of children.
6 Make sure the bowl or container is firmly in position before fitting any attachments, and before switching on.
7 Always use the plastic pusher when grating or slicing food – never push with your fingers.
8 Check that you have the correct attachment fitted before putting any food in the bowl.
9 When adding liquids to other ingredients, pour through the feed tube while the machine is running.
10 When you first use the machine, keep an eye on the ingredients you are processing, remembering that the machine works very fast.

*Type C, Moulinex
Food Preparation System*

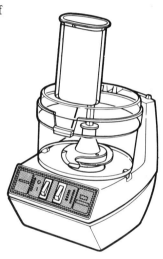

*Type D, Sona
Food Processor*

Care of your food processor

Do not immerse the motor base in water, simply wipe clean using a damp cloth. Wash the bowl or container and all the attachments in hot soapy water and rinse well (these can also go in a dish washer). Take care when drying to avoid touching the sharp blades.

The attachments and their uses

The double-bladed chopping knife

This metal chopping blade is probably the most versatile of all attachments, enabling you to chop, mix, beat, purée, mince, make breadcrumbs, pastry, bread and much more. However, care must be taken not to over-chop food – a few seconds too long could mean the difference between a chopped onion and a purée!

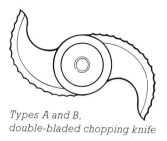

Types A and B, double-bladed chopping knife

Chopping Always cut the food into even-sized pieces before chopping in the machine, otherwise the food will be unevenly prepared. If the food is particularly hard, drop it through the feed tube onto the revolving blades, if the machine has this facility. If in any one recipe, there are several foods to be chopped, make sure that you do not over-chop at the beginning before adding the remaining ingredients.

The recipes in this book have been written so that the ingredients are chopped in the correct order to prevent having to wash up between processes.

When chopping herbs or making breadcrumbs, make sure the bowl and the herbs are completely dry, otherwise you could end up with a soggy mess!

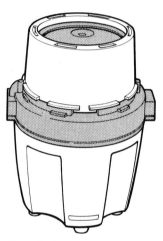

Type C, chopper

Puréeing Depending upon the type of machine, this process can be carried out using the double-bladed chopping knife (types A and B) or the chopper/blender (type C). This is ideal for making batters, baby foods, sauces, soups, pâtés, fruit and vegetable purées and for invalid dishes. It is important to check the quantity of food that the bowl or goblet will hold.

Type C, chopper/blender

Mincing or grinding The machine is invaluable for this, whether you want to mince raw or cooked food. Always make sure that the food is cut up evenly before putting into the machine, otherwise it will be unevenly processed.

Slicing and shredding attachments

Type A and B machines have separate slicing and grating discs, which are fitted onto the central spindle in the plastic bowl. The food is placed in the feed tube and pushed onto the revolving disc, using the plastic pusher as a guide. The more pressure you apply, the thicker the slice. The sliced food is collected in the plastic bowl, which is emptied as necessary (see diagram). If necessary, cut the food to fit into the feed tube.

Types A and B, processed food is collected in the bowl

Type C machines have a base which is fitted onto the motor with a delivery spout. The cutting discs are placed on top, and fastened into position with a screw nut. A cover is attached and locked onto the base. The food is placed in the feed tube and guided onto the revolving disc by a plastic pusher. The food is delivered straight into a container, making the process continuous (see diagram). With this type of machine, there is also a blade which enables you to prepare chipped potatoes.

These attachments are invaluable in the preparation of fruit and vegetables for freezing, and also in the making of preserves, eliminating all the tedious and time-consuming slicing.

Type C, sliced food is collected outside the machine

Type A such as Magimix

Stainless steel double-bladed knife
Use to chop fresh or raw food, purée, mince, make breadcrumbs, pastry, bread, sauces and batters. Use to make castor sugar from granulated and to crush ice.

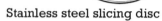

Plastic mixing blade
Use when ingredients are to be mixed rather than cut, e.g. cakes or mashed potatoes.

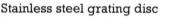

Stainless steel slicing disc
Use to slice vegetables and fruit.

Stainless steel grating disc
Use to grate vegetables, cheese, chocolate, etc.

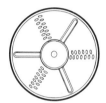

Also available as optional extras is a range of other blades and attachments – juice extractor, ripple cut disc, Parmesan grating disc, julienne slicing disc, French fried potato disc and coleslaw disc.

Type B such as Robot-Chef

Stainless steel double-bladed knife
Use to chop fresh or raw food, purée, mince, make breadcrumbs, pastry, bread, sauces and batters. Use to make castor sugar from granulated and to crush ice.

Stainless steel slicing disc
Use to slice vegetables and fruit.

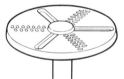

Stainless steel grating disc
Use to grate vegetables, cheese, chocolate, etc.

Also available as an optional extra is a French fried potato disc.

The chopper
Use to chop fresh or raw food, make breadcrumbs.

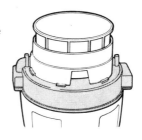

The chopper/blender
Use to make purées, cakes, sauces and batters.

The chopper/veg chef
Use for all slicing and grating of vegetables and fruit and for chipping potatoes.

Knife blade
Use to chop fresh or raw food, purée, mince, make breadcrumbs, pastry bread, sauces and batters and make castor sugar from granulated.

Reversible disc for slicing and shredding
Use to slice vegetables and fruit, and for grating vegetables, cheese, chocolate, etc.

Soups

There is nothing more welcoming than home-made soup, and the food processor really comes into its own for soup making. No more laborious chopping of vegetables and messy sieving – the machine takes care of it all.

The recipes in this chapter include some traditional soups, specially adapted to make the best use of the food processor, as well as some new ideas. Even left-over vegetables can be turned into a delicious soup in seconds.

▣ ▣ Crème de poisson

Clean the leeks and stand them vertically in the feed tube. Slice, using the slicing disc. Repeat this with the potatoes. Place the sliced vegetables in a saucepan with the stock and salt. Bring to the boil and simmer for 5–8 minutes. Add the tomatoes, cod and parsley and cook for a further 5 minutes. Allow to cool slightly then purée until smooth, using the double-bladed chopping knife. Stir in the milk, pepper and celery salt. Reheat and add the cream just before serving.

3 leeks
2 medium potatoes
1.15 litres/2 pints stock
salt
1 (227-g/8-oz) can
   tomatoes
225 g/8 oz cod
few sprigs parsley
300 ml/½ pint milk
freshly ground black
   pepper
pinch of celery salt
150 ml/¼ pint single
   cream

Serves 6

▣ Smoked haddock soup

Peel and quarter the potato and onion, and cut the raw fish into 2.5-cm/1-inch cubes. Place these ingredients in the bowl and chop finely, using the double-bladed chopping knife. Add the grated lemon rind and mix well.

Melt the butter and fry the chopped ingredients for a few minutes. Stir in the flour and add the stock, milk, dried herbs and turmeric.

Bring this to the boil, stirring continuously, and simmer for 30 minutes. Stir in the lemon juice and serve hot, garnished with parsley.

100 g/4 oz potato
½ medium onion
225 g/8 oz smoked
   haddock
grated rind and juice of
   ½ lemon
25 g/1 oz butter
25 g/1 oz flour
600 ml/1 pint vegetable
   stock
300 ml/½ pint milk
pinch of dried tarragon
1 teaspoon dried sweet
   basil
¼ teaspoon turmeric
Garnish
few sprigs parsley

Serves 4

◙ Tomato and carrot soup

Illustrated on page 19

1 small onion
175 g/6 oz carrots
450 g/1 lb tomatoes
50 g/2 oz butter
50 g/2 oz plain flour
1.15 litres/2 pints
  mixed herb stock,
  made with a stock cube
1 teaspoon castor sugar
1 teaspoon dried
  oregano
½ teaspoon paprika
½ teaspoon ground mace
2 tablespoons tomato
  purée
salt and freshly ground
  black pepper
6 tablespoons single
  cream
Serves 4–6

Peel and roughly slice the onion and carrots; peel and slice the tomatoes.

Place the onion and carrots in the bowl and chop roughly, using the double-bladed chopping knife. Add the sliced tomatoes and continue until the mixture is finely chopped.

Melt the butter in a saucepan and lightly sauté the chopped vegetables. Stir in the flour and add the stock, sugar, oregano, spices, tomato purée and seasonings. Bring to the boil and simmer gently for 30 minutes.

Pour the soup into the bowl and purée until smooth, using the double-bladed chopping knife. Reheat and serve hot in individual bowls with a tablespoon of single cream swirled on top of each.

◙ Split pea broth

175 g/6 oz yellow split
  peas
100 g/4 oz streaky
  bacon
1 medium onion
few sprigs parsley
1.15 litres/2 pints stock
300 ml/½ pint milk
salt and freshly ground
  black pepper

Serves 4

Cover the peas with water and leave to soak overnight. Drain.

Cut the bacon into 2.5-cm/1-inch pieces and place in the bowl. Chop finely using the double-bladed chopping knife and transfer to a saucepan.

Peel and quarter the onion and place in the bowl with the parsley. Chop finely, using the double-bladed chopping knife and add to the saucepan with the bacon. Fry the mixture gently in the bacon fat until the onion is transparent. Add the split peas, stock and milk. Season and bring to the boil, cover then simmer for 1 hour.

Pour the soup into the bowl and purée it, using the double-bladed chopping knife. Return to the pan and simmer for a further 30 minutes – 1 hour. Serve hot.

🔲 Cream of fennel soup

Illustrated on page 19

Trim and wash the fennel. Cut into quarters and cook in boiling salted water with the lemon juice until tender – about 30 minutes.

Drain the fennel and slice roughly. Melt the butter in a large saucepan and sauté the fennel for a few minutes. Stir in the flour, then add half the stock and milk, the ground mace and seasoning.

Finely chop the parsley, using the double-bladed chopping knife. Place the fennel and stock mixture in the bowl with the parsley and purée until smooth, using the double-bladed chopping knife. Return this mixture to the saucepan, add the remaining stock and milk and bring to the boil. Simmer gently, stirring occasionally for 10 – 15 minutes. Serve hot, garnished with a sprig of fennel.

2 heads of fennel, about 575 g / 1¼ lb
juice of ½ lemon
40 g / 1½ oz butter
40 g / 1½ oz plain flour
600 ml / 1 pint chicken stock, made with a stock cube
300 ml / ½ pint milk
½ teaspoon ground mace
salt and freshly ground black pepper
few sprigs parsley

Serves 4

◑ ◎ French onion soup

Illustrated opposite

450 g / 1 lb onions
50 g / 2 oz butter
1 tablespoon cooking oil
few sprigs parsley
900 ml / 1½ pints beef
  stock, made with
  2 stock cubes
1 teaspoon yeast extract
salt and freshly ground
  black pepper
4 slices French bread,
  sprinkled with grated
  cheese and grilled

Peel and halve the onions. Fit the slicing disc and feed the onions into the bowl to slice them.

Melt the butter and oil in a pan. Add the sliced onion and stir well. Leave over a low heat to brown.

Finely chop the parsley, using the double-bladed chopping knife.

Add the stock, yeast extract and parsley to the onion. Season to taste. Simmer the soup for 20 minutes. Serve hot in individual bowls with a slice of French bread on each.

Serves 4

◎ Country soup with frankfurters

Illustrated on the jacket

225 g / 8 oz carrots
225 g / 8 oz parsnips
1 medium onion
2 large sprigs parsley
40 g / 1½ oz butter
900 ml / 1½ pints stock
2 tablespoons tomato
  purée
1 teaspoon
  Worcestershire sauce
225 g / 8 oz frankfurters,
  sliced
salt and freshly ground
  black pepper

Peel the carrots and parsnips and cut into even-sized chunks. Peel and quarter the onion.

Place the vegetables and parsley in the bowl and chop roughly, using the double-bladed chopping knife. Melt the butter, add the vegetables to the pan and fry for 4 – 5 minutes. Add the stock, bring to the boil and simmer for 30 minutes. Stir in the tomato purée, Worcestershire sauce and sliced frankfurters. Season to taste, reheat and serve.

Serves 4

Cream of fennel soup (see page 17); French onion soup (see above); Tomato and carrot soup (see page 16)

Courgette and yogurt soup

Peel the onion and cut it into quarters. Place in the bowl and chop finely, using the double-bladed chopping knife.

Melt the butter and sauté the onion until soft but not browned.

Wash and trim the courgettes, then slice them thinly, using the slicing disc. Add to the pan and cook for 3–4 minutes. Stir in the stock, seasoning and nutmeg and simmer for 10 minutes. Cool slightly then purée, using the double-bladed chopping knife until smooth.

Return to the pan, stir in the milk and reheat. Serve in individual bowls with a tablespoon of natural yogurt in each. Sprinkle with chopped parsley.

1 onion
25 g/1 oz butter
1 kg/2 lb courgettes
900 ml/1½ pints chicken stock
salt and freshly ground black pepper
freshly grated nutmeg
300 ml/½ pint milk
1 (142-ml/5-fl oz) carton natural yogurt

Garnish
chopped parsley

Serves 6

Beetroot and orange soup

Halve the beetroot and chop finely, using the double-bladed chopping knife. Make up the orange juice according to the instructions on the can. Gradually add to the beetroot through the feed tube and purée until the mixture is smooth.

Pour the soup into a bowl, season to taste and chill in the refrigerator.

Whip the cream lightly in a small bowl and fold in the grated orange rind.

Stir the soup and serve in individual bowls with a tablespoon of cream floating on each.

Note Rinse the bowl and double-bladed chopping knife as soon as the beetroot mixture is removed, to avoid staining.

450 g/1 lb cooked beetroot, peeled
1 (178-g/6¼-fl oz) can concentrated orange juice
salt and freshly ground black pepper
4 tablespoons whipping cream
grated rind of ½ orange

Serves 4

Potted meat pâté (see page 30); Moules provençales (see page 25); Welsh leek flan (see page 60)

Cream of cucumber soup

1 onion
25 g/1 oz butter
25 g/1 oz flour
300 ml/½ pint chicken
   stock
1 cucumber
450 ml/¾ pint milk
salt and freshly ground
   black pepper
freshly grated nutmeg
pinch of cayenne
150 ml/¼ pint single
   cream

Serves 4

Peel and quarter the onion. Chop finely, using the double-bladed chopping knife.

Melt the butter and sauté the onion until soft but not browned. Stir in the flour and cook for 1 minute. Stir in the stock and bring to the boil, stirring all the time.

Peel the cucumber and chop roughly, using the double-bladed chopping knife. Stir the cucumber into the soup with the milk, seasoning, nutmeg and cayenne, and simmer for 5–10 minutes. Cool slightly then purée until smooth.

Chill thoroughly and stir in the cream just before serving.

Cucumber gazpacho

1 small onion, peeled
few sprigs parsley
1 sprig mint
1 clove garlic
1 cucumber
1 teaspoon lemon juice
½ teaspoon
   Worcestershire sauce
1 teaspoon wine vinegar
600 ml/1 pint tomato
   juice
salt and freshly ground
   black pepper
Garnish
ice cubes
croûtons

Serves 4

Place the onion, parsley, mint and garlic in the bowl and chop finely, using the double-bladed chopping knife.

Peel the cucumber and cut into 5-cm/2-inch lengths. Feed into the bowl until roughly chopped. Mix all the ingredients together and chill well. Float ice cubes on top and serve with croûtons.

Starters and appetisers

The food processor is an invaluable aid in the preparation of starters and appetisers. Pâtés can be made with the minimum of effort; the smooth texture achieved is beyond comparison with that obtained from other methods of preparation. Creamy, feather-light mousses and soufflés and short pastry can be made very successfully using the food processor.

▣ Fisherman's surprise

450 g / 1 lb potatoes
salt and freshly ground
  black pepper
175 g / 6 oz frozen cod or
  hake steaks,
  defrosted
few sprigs parsley
2 tablespoons single
  cream
grated rind of 1 lemon
2 eggs, separated
2 tablespoons natural
  yogurt

Serves 4

Peel the potatoes and boil until tender. Add seasoning and purée until smooth, using the double-bladed chopping knife. Spoon the potato from the bowl into a piping bag fitted with a large vegetable star nozzle.

Cut the defrosted fish steaks into chunks and place in the bowl with the parsley and cream. Add seasoning and the grated lemon rind and mix, using the double-bladed chopping knife.

Divide the mixture between 4 greased scallop shells or shallow, individual, ovenproof dishes. Pipe potato round the edge of each shell or dish.

Mix together the egg yolks and yogurt. Whisk the egg whites until stiff and fold into the egg yolk mixture with a metal spoon. Use this to cover the fish.

Bake in a moderately hot oven (200°C, 400°F, Gas Mark 6) for 20 minutes. Serve hot.

Moules provençales

Illustrated on page 20

Scrub the mussels well, removing the beards and discarding any open shells. Place the mussels in a steamer or a colander standing over a saucepan of boiling water and steam for 3 minutes until the shells are just opening. Discard any that do not open. Remove from the heat and break off the empty half of each shell.

Finely chop the onions and parsley, using the double-bladed chopping knife. Add the remaining ingredients and mix well. Spread a little of the mixture over each mussel. Just before serving place the mussels under a hot grill until lightly browned. Garnish with chopped parsley.

1.75 litres/3 pints
  mussels
3 spring onions
few sprigs parsley
100 g/4 oz butter
1–2 cloves garlic
40 g/1½ oz fresh
  breadcrumbs
salt and freshly ground
  black pepper
Garnish
chopped parsley

Serves 4

Little cheese and curry soufflés

Place the butter, flour and milk in the bowl and mix well, using the double-bladed chopping knife. Pour the mixture into a saucepan, add the seasoning and bring to the boil, stirring continuously. Cook the thickened mixture for 2 minutes.

Grate the cheese using the grating disc. Return the cooked sauce mixture to the bowl with the yolks, curry powder and grated cheese and mix until smooth.

Whisk the egg whites until stiff and fold into the mixture with a metal spoon.

Divide the mixture between 6 greased individual soufflé dishes. Sprinkle with paprika and grated Parmesan. Bake in a moderately hot oven (190°C, 375°F, Gas Mark 5) for 25 minutes. Serve hot.

25 g/1 oz butter
25 g/1 oz flour
150 ml/¼ pint milk
salt and freshly ground
  black pepper
100 g/4 oz Cheddar
  cheese
4 eggs, separated
1 teaspoon curry
  powder
paprika
grated Parmesan
  cheese

Serves 6

Watercress and cheese quiche

225 g/8 oz cheese
  pastry (see page 96)
1 medium onion
15 g/½ oz butter
1 bunch watercress,
  stalks removed
2 eggs
150 ml/¼ pint milk
salt and freshly ground
  black pepper
225 g/8 oz cottage
  cheese
freshly grated nutmeg

Serves 4 – 6

Roll out the pastry and use to line a 20-cm/8-inch flan ring. Bake blind in a moderately hot oven (200°C, 400°F, Gas Mark 6) for 15 minutes.

Peel and quarter the onion and chop finely, using the double-bladed chopping knife. Melt the butter in a saucepan and cook the onion in it until transparent.

Roughly chop the watercress, using the double-bladed chopping knife. Remove from the bowl and set aside.

Place the eggs, milk and seasoning in the bowl and mix together well, using the double-bladed chopping knife.

Mix the onion, watercress and cottage cheese and spread over the base of the partially cooked pastry case. Pour over the milk and egg mixture and sprinkle with freshly grated nutmeg. Bake in a moderate oven (180°C, 350°F, Gas Mark 4) for 20 – 30 minutes, or until the filling is set. Serve hot or cold.

Cheese puffs

125 g/4½ oz plain flour
¼ teaspoon salt
1 tablespoon cooking oil
6 tablespoons water
1 egg white
225 g/8 oz hard cheese
oil for deep frying

Serves 4 – 6

Sieve the flour and salt into the bowl. Using the double-bladed chopping knife, start mixing and gradually pour in the cooking oil and water through the feed tube. Continue until the batter is smooth and thick.

Whisk the egg white until stiff and fold into the batter with a metal spoon.

Cut the cheese into 1-cm/½-inch cubes, dip each in batter and deep fry, a few at a time, in hot fat. When puffy and golden brown, remove the puffs from the fat and drain on kitchen paper. Serve hot.

Mushroom gougères

Spoon the choux pastry into a piping bag fitted with a large, plain vegetable nozzle. Pipe a ring of the pastry around the inside of 6 greased, individual soufflé dishes. Bake in a hot oven (220°C, 425°F, Gas Mark 7) for 20 minutes.

Meanwhile, peel and slice the onion and roughly chop the bacon. Chop finely together, using the double-bladed chopping knife. Remove from the bowl and set aside.

Melt the butter in a saucepan and sauté the onion, bacon and mushrooms until tender. Stir in the flour and then add the milk and wine. Season, then simmer, stirring continuously, for 3 minutes.

When the choux cases are cooked, remove from the oven and fill the centres with the mushroom mixture. Finely chop the cheese, using the double-bladed chopping knife, and sprinkle it over the gougères. Return them to the oven for 5 – 10 minutes. Serve immediately.

cheese choux pastry
  made with 50 g/2 oz
  butter etc. (see
  page 96)
½ medium onion
25 g/1 oz bacon
50 g/2 oz mushrooms
50 g/2 oz butter
50 g/2 oz plain flour
250 ml/8 fl oz milk
2 tablespoons white
  wine
salt and freshly ground
  black pepper
40 g/1½ oz Cheddar
  cheese

Serves 6

Pork and spinach terrine

Illustrated on page 2

450 g/1 lb lean pork
1 onion
1 clove garlic
50 g/2 oz streaky bacon
3 tablespoons
  breadcrumbs
few sprigs fresh sage
few sprigs parsley
beaten egg, to mix
100 g/4 oz frozen leaf
  spinach, thawed
salt and freshly ground
  black pepper
150 ml/$\frac{1}{4}$ pint aspic jelly
Garnish
slice of orange
bay leaves
few juniper berries

Serves 4 – 6

Finely chop the pork, using the double-bladed chopping knife. Peel and quarter the onion then chop with the garlic and bacon. Add to the pork together with the breadcrumbs.

Using the double-bladed chopping knife, coarsely chop the herbs and stir into the meat. Add sufficient beaten egg to give a soft mixture.

Finely chop the spinach, using the double-bladed chopping knife and season well.

Place half the meat mixture in a 1-litre/1$\frac{1}{2}$-pint terrine, then add the chopped spinach and finish with the remaining meat, packing down well. Cover and place the terrine in a baking tin, half filled with water. Bake in a moderate oven (180°C, 350°F, Gas Mark 4) for 1$\frac{1}{4}$ – 1$\frac{1}{2}$ hours. Allow to cool.

Make up the aspic jelly and pour over the terrine. Garnish with a slice of orange, bay leaves and a few juniper berries.

Ham moulds

Cook the rice in twice its volume of salted water until all the water has been absorbed. Drain the rice and allow to cool.

Mix the butter, flour, milk, seasoning, tomato purée, Tabasco sauce and mustard until smooth, using the double-bladed chopping knife. Transfer the mixture to a saucepan and bring to the boil, stirring continuously. Simmer, while stirring, for 2–3 minutes and set aside to cool.

Halve the hard-boiled egg and chop roughly, using the double-bladed chopping knife. Remove the egg from the bowl and set aside.

Cut the ham into pieces, and chop finely with the parsley, using the double-bladed chopping knife.

Pour the sauce into a mixing bowl with the egg, rice, ham and parsley, and mix well.

Place a slice of cucumber in the base of each of 6 greased dariole moulds. Divide the ham mixture between the moulds, pressing it down firmly, and leave to set in the refrigerator.

To turn the moulds out, dip each one quickly into hot water. Serve on a bed of chopped watercress with Melba toast.

50 g/2 oz long-grain rice
50 g/2 oz butter
50 g/2 oz plain flour
300 ml/$\frac{1}{2}$ pint milk
salt and freshly ground black pepper
2 tablespoons tomato purée
few drops of Tabasco sauce
$\frac{1}{4}$ teaspoon made mustard
1 egg, hard-boiled
225 g/8 oz ham
few sprigs parsley
6 thin slices cucumber

To serve
watercress
Melba toast

Serves 6

🌀 Potted meat pâté

Illustrated on page 20

225 g/8 oz belly pork
225 g/8 oz veal
100 g/4 oz chicken
  livers
100 g/4 oz streaky
  bacon
1 clove garlic
few sprigs parsley
10 juniper berries
¼ teaspoon mustard seed
freshly ground nutmeg
salt and freshly ground
  black pepper
grated rind of ½ lemon
1 tablespoon brandy
1 tablespoon red wine

Serves 4 – 6

Using the double-bladed chopping knife, finely chop the pork, veal, chicken livers, bacon, garlic and parsley. Crush the juniper berries and mustard seed in a mortar or with a rolling pin.

Mix all the ingredients together and place in a greased 0.75-litre/1-pint soufflé dish. Cover with foil and stand in a baking tin two-thirds filled with water. Bake in a moderate oven (180°C, 350°F, Gas Mark 4) for 1 – 1¼ hours.

Allow to cool and place weights on top. Chill overnight.

🌀 Cheese mousse in bread cases

small bunch fresh
  chives
40 g/1½ oz butter
40 g/1½ oz plain flour
300 ml/½ pint milk
¼ teaspoon made
  mustard
salt and freshly ground
  black pepper
2 eggs, separated
75 g/3 oz Stilton cheese
75 g/3 oz cream cheese
15 g/½ oz gelatine
1 medium sliced loaf of
  brown bread
butter for spreading

Serves 10 – 12

Finely chop the chives, using the double-bladed chopping knife. Put the butter, flour, milk, mustard and seasoning in the bowl with the chives and mix well, using the double-bladed chopping knife. Pour this mixture into a saucepan and bring to the boil gradually, stirring all the time. Simmer gently for 2 – 3 minutes, then cool slightly and beat in the egg yolks.

Mix the cheeses together until smooth using the double-bladed chopping knife. Dissolve the gelatine in 3 tablespoons of hot water. Whisk the egg whites until stiff.

Add the sauce to the bowl with the cheeses and mix well, using the double-bladed chopping knife. Pour the dissolved gelatine into the mixture through the feed tube, mixing all the time.

Transfer this to a mixing bowl and fold in the whisked egg whites with a metal spoon. Leave the mousse in the refrigerator to set.

Remove the crusts from the bread. Roll each slice of bread with a rolling pin until it is soft and pliable. Using a plain 8.5-cm/3½-inch round cutter, cut 25 rounds of bread. Butter these on both sides and press each one into a patty tin. Bake in a moderately hot oven (200°C, 400°F, Gas Mark 6) for 20 minutes or until golden brown. Leave in the tins to cool, then remove and fill with the cheese mousse mixture. Serve immediately.

▣ Chicken terrine

Clean the mushrooms and quarter the onion. Place them in the bowl with the bread and parsley and chop finely, using the double-bladed chopping knife. Transfer to a mixing bowl.

Remove the flesh from the chicken and chop finely together with the chicken livers, using the double-bladed chopping knife. Combine this with the breadcrumb mixture and add all the remaining ingredients except the bacon. Stretch the bacon rashers on a board, using the back of a knife. Use the rashers to line a 1-kg/2-lb loaf tin. Turn the chicken mixture into the lined loaf tin and cover the top with foil. Stand this in a baking tin two-thirds filled with water. Bake in a moderate oven (180°C, 350°F, Gas Mark 4) for 1½–2 hours. Allow to cool and chill well before serving.

100 g/4 oz mushrooms
1 onion, peeled
2 slices white bread
few sprigs parsley
1 (1.5-kg/3¼-lb) chicken
100 g/4 oz chicken livers
1 tablespoon freshly chopped tarragon
1 egg, beaten
1 tablespoon cream
1 tablespoon red wine
grated rind of ½ lemon
7 rashers streaky bacon

Serves 6

Fish

Seafood is often neglected, but with a
little imagination and the help of a food
processor, it can be turned into an
appealing dish for the family or guests.
You can use fresh or smoked fish,
shellfish on its own or added to fish, with
unusual sauces such as Stilton sauce with
skate or a green mayonnaise with
croquettes. A tasty sauce or stuffing will
enhance any fish dish and make it your
main choice for a meal.

◨ Stuffed mackerel en chemise

Remove the heads from the mackerel and gut by slitting along the underside with a sharp knife. With the flesh side down, press along the backbone using the thumb. Turn the mackerel over and remove the backbone. Wash the fish and dry well. Spread the mustard inside each fish.

Make the breadcrumbs, using the double-bladed chopping knife, then add the onion, parsley sprigs, lemon rind and seasoning to the bowl and chop. Pour in sufficient beaten egg through the feed tube to bind the mixture. Fill the fish with the stuffing.

Roll out the pastry thinly into an oblong 2.5 cm/1 inch longer than the fish. Cut in half and wrap each fish in the pastry, sealing the edges with beaten egg and tucking the ends underneath. Place on a damp baking tray and make three slashes across the top of each fish. Brush with beaten egg and bake in a hot oven (220°C, 425°F, Gas Mark 7) for 20 minutes, then reduce the oven to moderately hot (190°C, 375°F, Gas Mark 5) for a further 15–20 minutes.

2 mackerel
2 teaspoons French mustard
4 slices white bread, crusts removed
1 onion
few sprigs parsley
grated rind of $\frac{1}{2}$ lemon
salt and freshly ground black pepper
beaten egg to bind
1 (212-g/7$\frac{1}{2}$-oz) packet puff pastry

Serves 4

▣ ▣ ▣ Seafood roulade

2 slices white bread
175 g/6 oz Dutch cheese
150 ml/$\frac{1}{4}$ pint single
  cream
salt and freshly ground
  black pepper
4 eggs, separated

Filling
40 g/1$\frac{1}{2}$ oz butter
40 g/1$\frac{1}{2}$ oz flour
300 ml/$\frac{1}{2}$ pint milk
75 g/3 oz prawns
salt and freshly ground
  black pepper
chopped parsley

Serves 4

Make breadcrumbs, using the double-bladed chopping knife. Grate the cheese, using the grating disc. Return the breadcrumbs to the bowl with the cheese and add the cream, seasoning and egg yolks. Mix well for a few seconds only.

Whisk the egg whites and fold into the cheese mixture with a metal spoon. Place in a greased and lined Swiss roll tin and smooth out evenly. Bake in a moderately hot oven (200°C, 400°F, Gas Mark 6) for 10 – 15 minutes. For the filling melt the butter and stir in the flour. Cook over a low heat for 1 minute, stirring all the time. Stir in the milk gradually, then bring to the boil. Add the prawns, seasoning and parsley and heat through.

Turn the roulade out onto greaseproof paper, quickly spread the filling over and roll up like a Swiss roll.

◙ Fish curry

Peel and quarter the onion and chop finely with the apple, using the double-bladed chopping knife.

Melt the butter in a large saucepan and fry the onion and apple gently for a few minutes. Stir in the flour, curry powder, spices and coconut. Cook for a few minutes, then gradually stir in the stock and cider. Cut the fish into 2.5-cm/1-inch cubes and add to the mixture with the Tabasco and chutney. Season to taste. Bring the curry to the boil and simmer gently for 15–20 minutes.

Just before serving, stir in the drained tropical fruit salad. Adjust the seasoning, reheat and serve hot with boiled rice.

Variation

For a special occasion, treat yourself to a prawn curry – substitute 675 g/1½ lb fresh, peeled prawns for the coley, reserve a few prawns for garnish. Simmer for only 10 minutes. Serve with saffron rice.

1 medium onion
1 apple, peeled
50 g/2 oz butter
50 g/2 oz flour
1 tablespoon curry powder
1 teaspoon ground coriander
1 teaspoon ground mustard seed
¼ teaspoon ground turmeric
2 tablespoons desiccated coconut
300 ml/½ pint stock
150 ml/¼ pint dry cider
675 g/1½ lb coley steaks
few drops of Tabasco sauce
1 tablespoon mango chutney
salt and freshly ground black pepper
1 (454-g/16-oz) can tropical fruit salad

Serves 4

◎ Croquettes and green mayonnaise

450 g / 1 lb mixed fish
  (shrimps, cod,
  smoked haddock),
  cooked
40 g / 1½ oz butter
40 g / 1½ oz flour
300 ml / ½ pint milk
1 egg yolk
2 tablespoons chopped
  parsley
salt and freshly ground
  black pepper
beaten egg
breadcrumbs
deep fat for frying

To serve

green mayonnaise (see
  page 74)

Serves 4

Remove any skin and bones from the fish and then chop, using the double-bladed chopping knife.

Place the butter, flour and milk in a saucepan and bring to the boil, whisking all the time. Allow to cool slightly then beat in the egg yolk, parsley, seasoning and fish. Spread the mixture on a plate and chill thoroughly. Divide the mixture into 8 and shape into croquettes. Coat the croquettes with egg and breadcrumbs. Heat the oil to 185°C/360°F or until a cube of day-old bread turns golden. Fry the croquettes for 5–6 minutes and drain well. Serve hot with green mayonnaise.

Variation

The same mixture can be served as a hot savoury – form the mixture into about 30 small balls and coat each one with beaten egg and breadcrumbs. Fry a few at a time, as above, keeping the cooked ones hot. Serve with the green mayonnaise as a dip.

◙ Cod mimosa

Peel and finely chop the onions, using the double-bladed chopping knife. Fry in the oil until soft, but not golden. Stir in the cod and split peas and cook for 2 minutes. Add the parsley, wine vinegar, garlic and seasoning. Cook for a further 2–3 minutes. Place in a serving dish and scatter with olives. Coarsely chop the hard-boiled eggs, using the double-bladed chopping knife. Sprinkle over the fish and garnish with chopped parsley. Serve hot.

Note This is a dish which is particularly popular with children. If preparing this dish for children, remember to remove or reduce the garlic and replace the olives with wedges of tomato.

3 onions
2 tablespoons oil
675 g/1½ lb cod, cooked and flaked
100 g/4 oz split peas, soaked overnight and cooked
2 tablespoons chopped parsley
2 teaspoons white wine vinegar
1 clove garlic, crushed
salt and freshly ground black pepper
18 black olives
3 eggs, hard-boiled
Garnish
chopped parsley

Serves 4

◕ ◔ Skate with Stilton cheese sauce

4 pieces wing of skate,
    about 225 g/8 oz each
450 ml/¾ pint stock,
    made with a mixed
    herb stock cube
75 g/3 oz butter
75 g/3 oz plain flour
300 ml/½ pint milk
salt and freshly ground
    black pepper
2 tablespoons tartare
    sauce
100 g/4 oz Stilton cheese

Garnish

parsley
wedges of lemon

Serves 4

Poach the skate in the stock in a large saucepan until tender, this will take about 20 minutes. Strain the fish carefully and reserve the stock. Keep the fish hot. Melt the butter in a saucepan and stir in the flour to form a roux. Cook for 1 minute then gradually stir in 300 ml/½ pint of the reserved herb stock and the milk. Season and bring to the boil gently, stirring all the time. Cook for 2–3 minutes. Stir in the tartare sauce.

Grate the Stilton, using the grating disc, and stir it into the sauce. Adjust the seasoning and reheat the sauce, but do not allow it to boil. Chop the parsley, using the double-bladed chopping knife. Serve the fish and the sauce hot, garnished with the parsley and wedges of lemon.

Note This is an ideal dinner party dish, making a change from the traditional skate au beurre noir. Ideal accompaniments to this dish could be baby carrots, tossed in butter and lemon juice, green beans, courgettes or broccoli spears.

◙ Smoked haddock moussaka

Peel and finely chop the onions, using the double-bladed chopping knife. Sauté in the oil until soft but not golden. Add the tomatoes, seasoning, parsley and cayenne and cook for 5 minutes. Roughly chop the smoked haddock and stir it into the pan. Cook gently for 5 minutes.

Slice the aubergines, sprinkle with salt and leave for 30 minutes. Rinse well and drain. Fry the aubergines in the oil for about 5 minutes. Layer the fish and aubergines alternately in an ovenproof dish, finishing with a layer of aubergines. Combine the eggs and yogurt and pour over the aubergines. Bake in a moderate oven (180°C, 350°F, Gas Mark 4) for 20 – 25 minutes. Garnish with chopped parsley and wedges of lemon.

2 small onions
1 tablespoon oil
1 (425-g/15-oz) can
  tomatoes
salt and freshly ground
  black pepper
1 tablespoon chopped
  parsley
pinch of cayenne
450 g/1 lb smoked
  haddock
3 aubergines
3 tablespoons oil
2 eggs, beaten
1 (142-ml/5-fl oz) carton
  natural yogurt

Garnish
chopped parsley
wedges of lemon

Serves 4

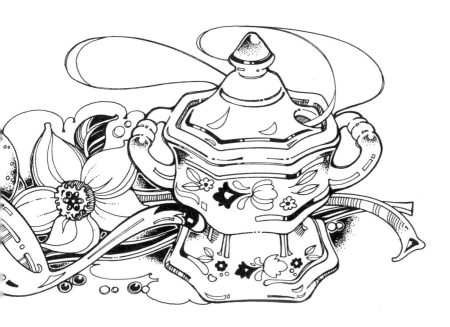

Kipper dauphinoise

1 onion
25 g / 1 oz butter
25 g / 1 oz flour
150 ml / $\frac{1}{4}$ pint milk
1 teaspoon lemon juice
grated rind of $\frac{1}{2}$ lemon
350 g / 12 oz kipper
  fillets, cooked and
  flaked
pinch of cayenne
salt and freshly ground
  black pepper
pinch of nutmeg
175 g / 6 oz cheese
2 eggs, hard-boiled
1 (227-g / 8-oz) packet
  frozen leaf spinach
2 medium potatoes

Serves 4

Peel and finely chop the onion, using the double-bladed chopping knife. Fry the onion in the butter until soft but not golden. Stir in the flour and cook for 1 minute, stirring all the time. Add the milk and bring to the boil. Stir in the lemon juice, rind, flaked fish, cayenne, seasoning and nutmeg. Turn the mixture into an ovenproof dish. Grate the cheese, using the grating disc and sprinkle half the cheese over the fish. Roughly chop the hard-boiled eggs, using the double-bladed chopping knife, and sprinkle over the cheese. Roughly chop the spinach in the same way as the eggs, and use it to cover the layer of egg. Peel the potatoes and pass them through the feed tube onto the slicing disc, using the plastic pusher. Blanch the sliced potatoes in boiling salted water for 5 – 8 minutes. Drain well and arrange overlapping on top of the spinach. Sprinkle with the remaining cheese and bake in a moderately hot oven (200°C, 400°F, Gas Mark 6) for 25 – 35 minutes.

meat, poultry and game

Whether you are using the cheaper or
more expensive cuts of meat, the food
processor is there to help you. Using the
double-bladed chopping knife or the
chopper/blender attachments, pâtés can
be made with complete ease and in the
minimum of time.

By preparing your own minced meats
you can be assured that the proportion of
fat to lean is not too high and that the
meat juices are retained, whereas in a
mincer they tend to be lost. Packs
prepared for the freezer will be
invaluable for all your favourite minced
dishes – spaghetti bolognese, moussaka
and hamburgers.

The food processor is also ideal for
making stuffings to complement veal,
lamb, pork and poultry dishes.

◙ Pasta bolognese

3 sticks of celery
2 carrots
1 onion
1 clove garlic
25 g/1 oz butter
2 tablespoons oil
350 g/12 oz chuck steak
· 225 g/8 oz lamb's liver
1 (396-g/14-oz) can
   tomatoes
3 tablespoons red wine
few drops of Tabasco
   sauce
salt and freshly ground
   black pepper
3 tablespoons chopped
   parsley

Serves 4−6

Finely chop the vegetables and garlic, using the double-bladed chopping knife. Sauté in the butter and oil until soft.

Chop the meat and liver, using the double-bladed chopping knife, and add to the sautéed vegetables. Mix in the remaining ingredients, cover and simmer for 1 hour. Serve with tagliatelle or spaghetti.

◙ Veal fricadelles in cream sauce

450 g/1 lb veal
50 g/2 oz ham
few sprigs parsley
1 egg
salt and freshly ground
   black pepper
25 g/1 oz butter
1 tablespoon oil
5 − 6 sprigs fresh basil
   or tarragon
150 ml/¼ pint white wine
150 ml/¼ pint double
   cream
25 g/1 oz butter

Serves 4−6

Trim the veal, removing any fat. Finely chop the veal, ham and parsley together, using the double-bladed chopping knife. Add the egg and seasoning and mix well. Shape into rounds about 1 cm/½ inch thick. Dredge the rounds with flour, shaking off any excess. Heat the butter and oil and seal the veal patties on both sides. Fry for 15 minutes, turning once during cooking.

Finely chop the basil using the double-bladed chopping knife. Add half the chopped basil to the wine in a pan and bring to the boil. Reduce to about 4 tablespoons then pour in the cream and heat until slightly thickened. Remove from the heat, beat in the butter and remaining basil and pour over the veal.

Pâté pie

Illustrated on the jacket

Roll out three-quarters of the pastry into a round to line the base and sides of an 18-cm/7-inch cake tin. Roll the remaining pastry into a round to use as a lid, reserving a little for decoration.

Cut the chicken into 2.5-cm/1-inch pieces and mince, using the double-bladed chopping knife.

Remove from the bowl and set aside. Remove the skin from the liver, peel and quarter the onion and mince together with the parsley and whole egg, using the double-bladed chopping knife. Turn this mixture into a mixing bowl and stir in the breadcrumbs, tomato purée and seasoning.

Use one-third of the liver mixture to make a layer in the base of the pastry-lined tin. Mix the whole hazelnuts with the chicken and use this to make a second layer in the pastry case. Make another layer with half of the remaining liver mixture. Mix the sausagemeat and sage together and season well. Form a fourth layer with the sausagemeat and finish with the remaining liver mixture. Brush the edges of the pastry with water and cover with the pastry lid, pressing the edges together to seal. Make a hole in the centre of the pie for steam to escape, use the remaining pastry pieces for decoration and brush all over with lightly beaten egg white. Cook in a moderately hot oven (200°C, 400°F, Gas Mark 6) for 30 minutes then reduce the oven temperature to moderate (180°C, 350°F, Gas Mark 4) for a further $1-1\frac{1}{2}$ hours.

Allow the pie to cool in the tin. Turn out and serve cold with salad and French bread.

275 g/10 oz hot water crust pastry (see page 97)
225 g/8 oz raw chicken flesh
225 g/8 oz pig's liver
1 medium onion
few sprigs parsley
1 egg
5 tablespoons fresh breadcrumbs
1 tablespoon tomato purée
salt and freshly ground black pepper
50 g/2 oz shelled hazelnuts
225 g/8 oz pork sausagemeat
$\frac{1}{2}$ teaspoon dried sage
1 egg white

Serves 8 – 10

▨ ◖ Olive pork pie

350 g/12 oz plain flour
pinch of salt
175 g/6 oz margarine
3 tablespoons water
1 large onion, peeled
2 tablespoons oil
225 g/8 oz lean pork
50 g/2 oz streaky bacon
350 g/12 oz sausagemeat
100 g/4 oz stuffed olives
beaten egg to glaze

Serves 6

Illustrated opposite

Mix the flour, salt and margarine together, using the double-bladed chopping knife, until the mixture resembles fine breadcrumbs. Add the water and mix to form a dough. Remove from the bowl and knead lightly on a floured surface. Divide the dough into 2 and leave one half in a cool place. Roll out the other half on a floured surface and use it to line a 19-cm/7½-inch square baking tin. Set aside in a cool place.

Quarter the onion and chop finely, using the double-bladed chopping knife. Heat the oil in a pan and fry the onion until tender but not brown. Cut the pork into 2.5-cm/1-inch cubes and mix, using the double-bladed chopping knife, until finely ground. Add to the onion. Finely chop the bacon in the same way and add to the pork mixture. Mix the sausagemeat to a smooth paste, using the double-bladed chopping knife. Mix this into the rest of the meat. Fry this mixture in its own fat until it is almost cooked and will break into pieces. Remove from the heat and cool slightly. Roughly slice the olives, using the slicing disc, and stir into the meat mixture. Use this to fill the pastry-lined tin. Roll out the rest of the pastry as a lid for the pie; brush the edges of the pastry with water and seal the lid on. Make a small hole in the top of the pie to let steam escape, then brush all over with beaten egg. Bake in a moderately hot oven (200°C, 400°F, Gas Mark 6) for 35–40 minutes. Serve hot or cold.

Olive pork pie (see above)

Overleaf: French lamb roast (see page 50)

◙ Steak tartare

Peel and quarter the onion and chop finely, using the double-bladed chopping knife. Roughly chop the meat, then chop until coarsely ground, using the double bladed chopping knife. Mix in the chopped onion, egg yolk, Tabasco sauce and seasoning.

Divide the meat into 4 patties and make a depression in the centre of each. Place an egg yolk in each depression and sprinkle with chopped parsley. Serve with small bowls of finely chopped spring onions, capers and anchovies.

1 onion
450 g / 1 lb lean beef
1 egg yolk
few drops of Tabasco
    sauce
salt and freshly ground
    black pepper
4 egg yolks
chopped parsley
To serve
finely chopped spring
    onions
chopped capers
chopped anchovies

Serves 4

◙ Peppered burgers

Illustrated opposite
Chop the bread, onion and parsley together, using the double-bladed chopping knife. Set aside. Trim the meat and mince together with the bacon, using the double-bladed chopping knife. Return the chopped onion mixture to the bowl and season. Add the beaten egg and mix together. Shape the mixture into 4 burgers. Crush the peppercorns in a pestle and mortar and press into the burgers.

Heat the butter and oil in a frying pan and fry the burgers 10 – 15 minutes, turning once during cooking. Drain well and serve with spicy tomato sauce.

1 slice bread
1 onion
few sprigs parsley
225 g /½ lb braising or
    chuck steak
2 rashers bacon, rinds
    removed
salt
1 egg, beaten
1 tablespoon black
    peppercorns
25 g / 1 oz butter
1 tablespoon pure corn
    oil
To serve
spicy tomato sauce (see
    page 81)

Serves 4

Peppered burgers (see above)

◖ ◗ French lamb roast

2 courgettes
2 onions
1 green pepper
225 g/8 oz mushrooms,
  cleaned
4 tomatoes, peeled
1 – 2 cloves garlic,
  crushed
3 tablespoons chopped
  parsley
salt and freshly ground
  black pepper
1 (1.5-kg/3¼-lb) leg of
  lamb

Serves 4

Illustrated on pages 46 – 7
Wash and trim the courgettes and slice,
using the slicing disc. Peel and quarter
the onions, wash the pepper and remove
the seeds. Roughly chop the onions,
peppers, mushrooms and tomatoes
together, using the double-bladed
chopping knife. Combine this with the
courgettes, garlic, parsley and
seasoning and use this mixture to cover
the base of a roasting tin. Place the lamb
on top, cover and bake in a moderately
hot oven (200°C, 400°F, Gas Mark 6) for
1¼ – 1½ hours. Serve with the cooked
vegetables.

◖ Pork boulangère

1 (1.5-kg/3¼-lb) loin of
  pork, rolled
few sprigs fresh
  rosemary
675 g/1½ lb potatoes,
  peeled
1 clove garlic, crushed
salt and freshly ground
  black pepper
75 g/3 oz butter
Garnish
chopped parsley
watercress

Serves 4

Illustrated on the jacket
Make small slits in the skin of the pork
using a sharp knife and insert a few
sprigs of fresh rosemary.
  Cut the potatoes in half and slice, using
the slicing disc. Arrange some of the
potatoes in the base of a casserole dish
and spread over the crushed garlic.
Sprinkle with a few more sprigs of
rosemary and place the pork on top.
Add the remaining potatoes around the
sides of the meat. Season and dot with
butter. Cover and cook in a moderate
oven (180°C, 350°F, Gas Mark 4) for
1¼ hours. Uncover and increase the oven
temperature to moderately hot (200°C,
400°F, Gas Mark 6) for a further 30 – 40
minutes to crisp the outside. Sprinkle the
potatoes with the parsley and garnish
with a bunch of watercress.

Cabbage parcel

Blanch the cabbage leaves in boiling, salted water for 1 minute. Drain well and use to line the base and sides of a 1-kg/ 2-lb loaf tin, reserving one leaf for the top.

Mince the meat, using the double-bladed chopping knife. Add the remaining ingredients and mix again until well combined. Turn the meat mixture into the lined tin, folding the cabbage leaves over to enclose the filling.

Place in a baking tin half filled with water. Cover with foil and bake in a moderate oven (180°C, 350°F, Gas Mark 4) for 1 – 1¼ hours. Drain off any liquid, turn out and garnish with slices of tomato. Serve hot with tomato sauce.

Note Serve cold with a salad if preferred.

4 – 6 large cabbage leaves
450 g / 1 lb chuck steak
150 ml / ¼ pint tomato juice
1 teaspoon Worcestershire sauce
few drops of Tabasco sauce
3 tablespoons tomato purée
100 g / 4 oz mushrooms
100 g / 4 oz breadcrumbs
1 egg
salt and freshly ground black pepper

Garnish
slices of tomato

To serve
spicy tomato sauce (see page 81)

Serves 4

◙ Ballotine of chicken

1 (1.5-kg/3¼-lb) chicken
Stuffing
1 onion, peeled
25 g/1 oz butter
225 g/8 oz ham
100 g/4 oz lean pork
50 g/2 oz walnuts
100 g/4 oz mushrooms
few sprigs fresh
  tarragon
few sprigs parsley
grated rind of ½ lemon
1 egg, beaten
15 g/½ oz pistachio nuts,
  blanched and skinned
salt and freshly ground
  black pepper
Topping
2 slices white bread
few sprigs parsley
2 tablespoons grated
  Parmesan cheese
1 clove garlic, crushed

Serves 4–6

Bone the chicken, taking care not to slit or cut the skin. Lay the boned chicken on a board, skin side downwards.

Quarter the onion and chop finely, using the double-bladed chopping knife. Sauté in the butter until tender. Finely chop the ham and pork, using the double-bladed chopping knife, and add to the sautéed onion. Coarsely chop the walnuts and mushrooms with the herbs and stir into the meat mixture. Add the remaining ingredients and mix well.

Spread the stuffing over the chicken and shape into a roll, sewing up the edges of the chicken to enclose the stuffing.

To make the topping, make the bread into breadcrumbs, using the double-bladed chopping knife, then add a few sprigs of parsley and chop finely. Stir in the Parmesan cheese and crushed garlic. Spread a little butter all over the chicken and then sprinkle with the topping. Place in a baking tin with a tablespoon of oil.

Bake in a moderately hot oven (190°C, 375°F, Gas Mark 5) for 1–1½ hours. Serve hot or cold.

◙ Stuffed pheasant with grapes

Remove the liver from the pheasant and mix with the walnuts and cream cheese until smooth, using the double-bladed chopping knife. Season and use to stuff the bird. Secure the opening with a skewer or sew up. Spread the butter all over the bird and lay the bacon across the breast. Place in a roasting tin and roast in a moderately hot oven (200°C, 400°F, Gas Mark 6) for 35–45 minutes, basting frequently. Five minutes before the end of the cooking time add the grapes and baste well with the juices. Remove the bacon and garnish the pheasant with the watercress. Serve the grapes around the edge of the dish.

Serve with bread sauce, game chips and fried crumbs.

1 pheasant
75 g/3 oz walnuts
75 g/3 oz cream cheese
salt and freshly ground
    black pepper
25 g/1 oz butter
3 rashers streaky bacon
225 g/8 oz white grapes
Garnish
watercress
Accompaniments
bread sauce (see
    page 79)
game chips (see below)
fried crumbs

Serves 3–4

◙ Game chips

Illustrated on page 58

Peel the potatoes and slice thinly, using the slicing disc. Rinse and dry well on kitchen paper. Heat the oil to 185°C/360°F and fry the chips a few at a time until crisp and golden. Drain well on kitchen paper and serve hot with poultry and game dishes.

225 g/8 oz potatoes
oil for deep frying

Serves 4

Accompaniments Chart

Meat	Accompaniments
Beef	Horseradish sauce
Lamb	Fresh mint sauce (see page 80), mint jelly, onion sauce (see page 79), redcurrant jelly
Pork	Apple sauce (see page 80), sage and onion stuffing
Veal	Parsley and thyme stuffing

Poultry	
Chicken	Bacon rolls, chipolata sausages, bread sauce (see page 79), stuffing
Duck	Apple sauce (see page 80), sage and onion stuffing
Goose	Apple sauce (see page 80), sage and onion stuffing
Guineafowl	Bread sauce (see page 79)
Pigeon	As for duck
Rabbit (tame)	Bread sauce (see page 79), forcemeat stuffing
Turkey	Bread sauce (see page 79), chestnut or sausagemeat stuffing, bacon rolls, cranberry sauce (see page 80)

Game	
Grouse	Bread sauce (see page 79), fried crumbs, game chips (see page 53)
Hare (saddle)	Forcemeat stuffing, redcurrant jelly
Partridge	Bread sauce (see page 79), fried crumbs, game chips (see page 53)
Pheasant	As for partridge
Ptarmigan	As for partridge
Quail	As for partridge
Venison	Redcurrant jelly

Vegetables

Vegetables are often neglected, and end up as merely an accompaniment to the main dish. In this chapter I have tried to show how the food processor can turn a simple vegetable into a complete dish in its own right, such as the red cabbage casserole or the stuffed marrow. The slicing and grating attachments have the ability to make vegetables go a long way – the bulk obtained from a shredded cabbage is quite remarkable!

◐ ◓ ◔ Vegetable lasagne

225 g/8 oz aubergines
1 medium onion
2 sticks of celery
2 medium courgettes
600 ml/1 pint stock
50 g/2 oz plain flour
50 g/2 oz butter
300 ml/½ pint milk
¼ teaspoon celery salt
freshly ground black
   pepper
225 g/8 oz lasagne
175 g/6 oz Cheddar
   cheese

Serves 6 – 8

Peel and halve the aubergines, sprinkle them with salt and leave to sweat for 30 minutes.

Peel the onion, clean the celery and trim the courgettes. Rinse and dry the aubergines and slice, with the other prepared vegetables, using the slicing disc. Simmer the vegetables in the stock for 10 – 15 minutes, then strain and reserve 300 ml/½ pint of the stock. Cool the stock and pour together with the flour, butter, milk, celery salt and black pepper into the bowl and mix well until smooth, using the double-bladed chopping knife. Pour this sauce mixture into a pan, bring to the boil slowly, stirring all the time, then simmer for 2 minutes.

Meanwhile cook the lasagne in boiling salted water, according to the directions on the packet.

Place a layer of cooked lasagne in the base of a 1.5-litre/2½-pint ovenproof dish. Cover this with half the cooked vegetables and then a layer of sauce. Grate the cheese, using the grating disc and sprinkle half of it over the sauce. Repeat these layers, ending with a layer of sauce covered with the remaining grated cheese. Bake in a moderate oven (180°C, 350°F, Gas Mark 4) for 30 minutes. If necessary brown the cheese under the grill before serving.

Assorted vegetables

◐ ◑ Potatoes dauphinoise

Illustrated opposite

Peel the potatoes and slice, using the slicing disc. Grate the cheese, using the grating disc. Place alternate layers of potatoes and cheese in an ovenproof dish, adding seasoning and nutmeg between each layer. Pour over the cream and bake in a moderate oven (180°C, 350°F, Gas Mark 4) for 50–60 minutes. Sprinkle with chopped parsley and serve.

450 g / 1 lb potatoes
175 g / 6 oz Gruyère
 cheese
salt and freshly ground
 black pepper
freshly ground nutmeg
300 ml / $\frac{1}{2}$ pint single
 cream
Garnish
3 tablespoons chopped
 parsley

Serves 4

◐ ◑ Rosti

Illustrated opposite

Peel the potatoes and parboil for 5 minutes. Chop the bacon, using the double-bladed chopping knife and sauté in butter until soft but not crisp.

 Grate the potatoes, using the grating disc, season well then add to the bacon. Fry until crisp on both sides.

 Grate the cheese, using the grating disc and sprinkle it over the potatoes. Place under a hot grill to melt the cheese and serve sprinkled with the chopped parsley.

450 g / 1 lb potatoes
4 rashers bacon
25 g / 1 oz butter
salt and freshly ground
 black pepper
100 g / 4 oz cheese
Garnish
2 tablespoons chopped
 parsley

Serves 4

*Game chips (see page 53); Rosti (see above);
Potatoes dauphinoise (see above)*

◐ ◓ ◑ Welsh leek flan

225 g / 8 oz cheese pastry
  (see page 96)
3 leeks
25 g / 1 oz butter
50 g / 2 oz ham
2 eggs
150 ml / ¼ pint single
  cream
freshly ground nutmeg
salt and freshly ground
  black pepper
few sprigs parsley
75 g / 3 oz Gruyère
  cheese

Serves 4–6

Illustrated on page 20

Make the pastry and use to line a 20-cm /
8-inch flan ring. Bake blind in a
moderately hot oven (200°C, 400°F, Gas
Mark 6) for 15 minutes.

Clean the leeks and slice, using the
slicing disc. Sauté them in the butter for 5
minutes. Chop the ham finely, using the
double-bladed chopping knife, then add
the eggs, cream, nutmeg, seasoning and
parsley and mix together thoroughly.

Place the leeks in the base of the flan
and pour in the egg mixture.

Grate the cheese, using the grating
disc, then sprinkle over the flan. Bake in
a moderately hot oven (190°C, 375°F, Gas
Mark 5) for 30 – 40 minutes.

◓ ◐ ◑ Courgettes au gratin

1 small onion
1 clove garlic
50 g / 2 oz butter
675 g / 1½ lb courgettes
1 teaspoon lemon juice
salt and freshly ground
  black pepper
100 g / 4 oz Cheddar
  cheese
25 g / 1 oz breadcrumbs
Garnish
chopped parsley

Serves 4

Peel the onion and garlic and chop
roughly, using the double-bladed
chopping knife. Melt the butter and fry
the onion and garlic until soft, but not
browned.

Trim the courgettes, place in the feed
tube and slice, using the slicing disc.
Sauté them in the butter with the onion
for about 5 minutes. Add the lemon juice
and seasoning and place in an ovenproof
dish.

Grate the cheese, using the grating
disc, and mix together with the
breadcrumbs. Sprinkle this over the
courgettes and bake in a moderate oven
(180°C, 350°F, Gas Mark 4) for 30 – 35
minutes. Garnish with chopped parsley
and serve hot.

▣ ▣ Stuffed marrow

Cut the marrow in half lengthways and scoop out the seeds.

Peel the onion and clean the celery. Chop the onion and celery together, using the double-bladed chopping knife. Grate the cheese, using the grating disc.

Remove the core from the kidney, and chop finely together with the bacon, using the double-bladed chopping knife. Add all the remaining ingredients together with the onion, celery and cheese; mix well using the double-bladed chopping knife. Divide the mixture between the two halves of marrow, then put the two halves back together again, securing them with skewers. Wrap the marrow in foil and bake in a moderately hot oven (190°C, 375°F, Gas Mark 5) for 50–60 minutes. Serve hot.

1 (1-kg/2¼-lb) marrow
1 small onion
1 stick of celery
75 g/3 oz Cheddar cheese
100 g/4 oz pig's kidney
50 g/2 oz bacon
50 g/2 oz breadcrumbs
1 egg
1 clove garlic, crushed
1 tablespoon tomato purée
1 tablespoon red wine or stock
¼ teaspoon dried mixed herbs
salt and freshly ground black pepper

Serves 6

♣ ◎ Spinach and nutmeg croquettes

100 g/4 oz butter
100 g/4 oz plain flour
300 ml/½ pint milk
salt and freshly ground
  black pepper
50 g/2 oz Cheddar
  cheese
¼ teaspoon freshly
  grated nutmeg
450 g/1 lb spinach
1 egg, lightly beaten
4 tablespoons milk
75 g/3 oz breadcrumbs
oil for deep frying
To serve
spicy tomato sauce (see
  page 78)

Serves 4

Melt the butter in a large saucepan and stir in the flour. Cook for a few minutes, then gradually stir in the milk and continue cooking until very thick. Season and cook for a further 2 minutes. Grate the cheese, using the grating disc, and stir into the cooked mixture with the nutmeg. Leave to cool. Trim the spinach and cook in boiling salted water until just tender. Chop finely, using the double-bladed chopping knife. Beat the spinach into the cheese sauce, adjust the seasoning, then spread the mixture over the base of a greased Swiss roll tin to about 1 cm/½ inch thick. Chill until set firmly.

Mark the mixture into 9 squares, then roll each piece into a croquette shape on a lightly floured board. Mix the egg and milk together and dip each croquette in the mixture. Coat each one in breadcrumbs and leave in the refrigerator for at least 30 minutes to allow the coating to harden.

Heat the fat to 185°C/360°F and fry the croquettes until the coating is crisp. Serve immediately with spicy tomato sauce.

◘ Carrots in cream and wine sauce

Peel the carrots and slice, using the slicing disc. Trim the onions down to the bulb. Melt the butter and sauté the carrots and onions for 5 minutes. Stir in the sugar, seasoning, cayenne, oregano and white wine. Cover and simmer for 20 – 25 minutes. Just before serving, spoon the soured cream on top and sprinkle with the chopped parsley.

450 g / 1 lb carrots
2 bunches spring onions
50 g / 2 oz butter
1 tablespoon brown sugar
salt and freshly ground black pepper
pinch of cayenne
1 teaspoon dried oregano
150 ml / ¼ pint white wine
1 (142-ml / 5-fl oz) carton soured cream
Garnish
2 tablespoons chopped parsley

Serves 4

◘ ◙ Red cabbage casserole

Remove the coarse outer leaves of the cabbage, together with the thick stalk. Cut the cabbage into wedges which will fit into the feed tube and slice, using the slicing disc. Peel the onions and slice in the same way. Chop the apples, using the double-bladed chopping knife.

Place layers of cabbage, onion and apple in an ovenproof casserole dish. Add the remaining ingredients, cover and bake in a moderately hot oven (200°C, 400°F, Gas Mark 6) for 50 – 60 minutes.

1 kg / 2¼ lb red cabbage
2 onions
2 cooking apples, peeled and cored
2 tablespoons brown sugar
2 tablespoons orange juice
3 tablespoons red wine vinegar
150 ml / ¼ pint chicken stock
salt and freshly ground black pepper

Serves 6

◪ Beans provençal

Peel the onion and chop finely, using the double-bladed chopping knife. Remove from the bowl and set aside. Roughly chop the bacon and mushrooms, using the double-bladed chopping knife.

Melt the butter in a saucepan and lightly sauté the onion, bacon, mushrooms and crushed garlic until soft. Sprinkle with the flour, stir well and cook for a few minutes.

Strain the can of tomatoes and purée the fruit until smooth, using the double-bladed chopping knife. Add the purée to the mixture in the saucepan with the sauces and seasoning. Cook, stirring, for 5 minutes.

Meanwhile trim the French beans and cook in boiling salted water until tender – about 10 minutes. Toss the beans in the hot tomato sauce, sprinkle with the grated Parmesan and serve immediately.

1 small onion
50 g/2 oz streaky bacon
50 g/2 oz mushrooms
15 g/½ oz butter
1 clove garlic, crushed
15 g/½ oz plain flour
1 (396-g/14-oz) can tomatoes
few drops of Worcestershire sauce
few drops of Tabasco sauce
salt and freshly ground black pepper
450 g/1 lb French beans
grated Parmesan cheese

Serves 4

Salads

The food processor is an absolute boon
in the preparation of salads. Although
fresh, colourful salads can enhance a
meal, they can mean lengthy and
laborious preparation for the housewife.
The machine will deal with all the
chopping, shredding and grating in
seconds!
The whole effect of a salad can be
ruined by badly prepared vegetables,
but the food processor is not only rapid,
it also preserves the natural colour and
flavour of food.

◙ Egg and watercress mousse

25 g / 1 oz butter
25 g / 1 oz flour
300 ml / ½ pint milk
½ bunch watercress
salt and freshly ground
    black pepper
2 eggs, hard-boiled
2 eggs, separated
15 g / ½ oz gelatine
2 tablespoons water
Garnish
watercress

Serves 4 – 6

Mix together the butter, flour, milk and watercress, using the double-bladed chopping knife, until the watercress is finely chopped. Pour into a saucepan and bring to the boil, whisking all the time. Season to taste.

Chop the hard-boiled eggs, using the double-bladed chopping knife, and fold into the sauce. Beat in the egg yolks and cool.

Dissolve the gelatine in the water and stir into the cooled sauce. When on the point of setting, whisk the egg whites until stiff and fold into the mixture with a metal spoon. Pour into a lightly oiled 1.5-litre/2½-pint mould. Leave in a cool place to set. Turn out and garnish with watercress.

◙ ◘ Mushrooms à la grecque

1 onion, peeled
25 g / 1 oz butter
1 clove garlic, crushed
150 ml / ¼ pint white wine
225 g / 8 oz mushrooms
4 tomatoes, peeled
salt and freshly ground
    black pepper
Garnish
chopped parsley

Serves 4

Quarter the onion and chop finely, using the double-bladed chopping knife. Sauté in the butter until soft, add the crushed garlic and wine and bring to the boil.

Slice the mushrooms, using the slicing disc, then add to the wine. Simmer gently for 2 – 3 minutes. Cut the tomatoes into quarters and stir in with the mushrooms. Season to taste then chill thoroughly before serving. Garnish with chopped parsley.

◩ Greek rice salad

Cook the rice in the chicken stock for 15–20 minutes, until the stock is absorbed.

Peel the onion and chop finely with the pepper, cucumber, mushrooms and parsley, using the double-bladed chopping knife. Stir the chopped vegetables into the rice. Add 3–4 tablespoons of the French dressing to moisten the rice, then pack into a lightly oiled 20-cm/8-inch ring mould. Chill until firm. Turn out carefully and fill the centre with olives.

225 g/8 oz long-grain rice
425 ml/¾ pint chicken stock
1 small onion
½ green pepper, seeds removed
½ cucumber
75 g/3 oz button mushrooms
few sprigs parsley
French dressing (see page 81)

Garnish
green and black olives

Serves 4–6

◪ ◩ Courgette salad

Clean the mushrooms and slice thickly with the courgettes, using the slicing disc. Cut the garlic sausage into even strips. Mix the mushrooms, courgettes and garlic sausage together. Chop the parsley, using the double-bladed chopping knife. Add the lemon rind and juice, the oil, salt, sugar and mustard. Season well with pepper. Mix well until the ingredients are emulsified. Pour this dressing over the courgette mixture and toss well. Cover and leave to stand for about 1 hour. Cut the tomatoes in wedges and toss into the salad before serving.

100 g/4 oz button mushrooms
450 g/1 lb courgettes, thinly peeled
225 g/8 oz garlic sausage, in 1 piece
small bunch parsley
grated rind and juice of 1 lemon
5 tablespoons salad oil
½ teaspoon salt
1 teaspoon sugar
½ teaspoon dry mustard
freshly ground black pepper
3 tomatoes, peeled

Serves 4

Pasta salad

225 g / 8 oz pasta shapes
French dressing (see
   page 81)
1 small onion
50 g / 2 oz streaky bacon
15 g / ½ oz butter
50 g / 2 oz mushrooms
2 eggs, hard-boiled
2 tablespoons chopped
   parsley
1 tablespoon chopped
   chives
salt and freshly ground
   black pepper

Serves 4 – 6

Cook the pasta in boiling salted water until tender. Drain well and toss in French dressing. Set aside to cool.

Peel and quarter the onion and chop finely with the bacon, using the double-bladed chopping knife.

Melt the butter in a pan and gently sauté the onion and bacon. Roughly chop the mushrooms, using the double-bladed chopping knife, and add to the onion and bacon. Continue to fry this mixture gently until soft. Strain off any excess fat, then add the mixture to the pasta.

Roughly chop the hard-boiled eggs, using the double-bladed chopping knife. Stir into the pasta mixture together with the chopped herbs.

Season to taste and serve cold.

Spinach salad

450 g / 1 lb fresh spinach
1 bunch spring onions
salt and freshly ground
   black pepper
freshly grated nutmeg
2 eggs, hard-boiled
To serve
French dressing (see
   page 81)

Serves 4

Remove and discard any coarse stems from the spinach, then chop roughly, using the double-bladed chopping knife. Trim the spring onions and chop. Mix with the spinach and add seasoning and nutmeg to taste.

Chop the eggs, using the double-bladed chopping knife, and sprinkle over the spinach. Serve with French dressing.

◐ ☙ Sage Derby coleslaw

Roughly chop the cheese, using the double-bladed chopping knife. Transfer the cheese to a large mixing bowl. Chop the blanched almonds finely, using the double-bladed chopping knife, and add to the cheese. Peel the cucumber and chop roughly in the same way, and add to the mixing bowl.

Cut the cabbage into wedges which will pass through the feed tube, and slice finely, using the slicing disc. Cut the green pepper into quarters lengthways, remove the seeds and slice finely, using the slicing disc.

Add the cabbage and pepper to the cheese, almonds and cucumber in the mixing bowl.

Peel, core and quarter the apples. Slice, using the slicing disc and sprinkle liberally with lemon juice to prevent discoloration. Add to the cabbage mixture.

Stir the mayonnaise, seasoning and chopped parsley into the coleslaw and mix well.

75 g/3 oz Sage Derby
  cheese
50 g/2 oz blanched
  almonds
50 g/2 oz cucumber
350 g/12 oz white
  cabbage
1 green pepper
2 apples
little lemon juice
150 ml/¼ pint basic
  mayonnaise (see
  page 74)
salt and freshly ground
  black pepper
2 tablespoons chopped
  parsley

Serves 6–8

◙ Avocado and orange salad

few sprigs parsley
grated rind of 1 orange
3 tablespoons orange
  juice
1 tablespoon white wine
  vinegar
6 tablespoons oil
salt and freshly ground
  black pepper
2 ripe avocados
2 small pears

Serves 4

Illustrated on the jacket
Chop the parsley, using the double-bladed chopping knife. Add the grated orange rind, juice, vinegar, oil and seasoning. Mix well to form a smooth dressing, using the double-bladed chopping knife. Pour the dressing into a basin.

Cut the avocados lengthways, remove the stones and carefully scoop out the flesh, leaving the skins undamaged. Cut the flesh into small cubes, and add to the dressing.

Peel, core and quarter the pears. Chop the flesh into cubes and stir into the avocado and dressing. Divide this filling between the avocado shells and serve immediately.

◙ Crunchy Waldorf salad

½ cucumber
few sprigs parsley
75 g/3 oz walnuts
3 sticks of celery
4 apples
little lemon juice
150 ml/¼ pint basic
  mayonnaise (see
  page 74)
few crisp lettuce leaves
Garnish
watercress
shredded orange rind

Serves 4

Illustrated on the jacket
Peel the cucumber and chop roughly, using the double-bladed chopping knife, together with the parsley, walnuts and celery. Core the apples and chop roughly in the same way, adding a little lemon juice to prevent discoloration. Mix all the ingredients together with the mayonnaise.

Shred the lettuce and use to line a dish. Pile the salad on top and garnish with watercress and orange rind.

⑥ ⓝ Savoury apple baskets

Wipe the apples and core them without breaking through the base. Take a slice off the top of each apple and carefully scoop out the flesh to within 5 mm/¼ inch of the skin. Put the apple flesh in a basin and sprinkle with lemon juice.

Finely chop the celery and green pepper, using the double-bladed chopping knife. Flake the tuna and mix into the soured cream; add to the celery and green pepper in the bowl, together with all the remaining ingredients except the cheese. Mix well using the double-bladed chopping knife.

Divide the mixture between the hollowed-out apples. Grate the cheese using the grating disc and sprinkle over each 'basket' before serving.

4 large, crisp eating
    apples
lemon juice
½ stick of celery
¼ green pepper, seeds
    removed
1 (99-g/3½-oz) can tuna
    steak
5 tablespoons soured
    cream
1 tablespoon chopped
    parsley
¼ teaspoon mild curry
    powder
few drops of Tabasco
    sauce
salt and freshly ground
    black pepper
25 g/1 oz Double
    Gloucester cheese

Serves 4

ⓞ Cucumber salad

Peel the cucumber and slice thinly, using the slicing disc. Sprinkle the cucumber with salt and leave for 30 minutes – 1 hour. Rinse well and drain. Toss in the French dressing and chill. Just before serving, sprinkle with the chopped parsley and sprigs of dill and serve with soured cream.

1 cucumber
salt, to sprinkle
French dressing (see
    page 81)
3 tablespoons chopped
    parsley
2 sprigs fresh dill
soured cream

Serves 4

◙ Calypso tomatoes

4 large firm tomatoes
1 ripe avocado
75 g/3 oz cream cheese
25 g/1 oz chopped nuts
2 teaspoons chopped
  chives
1 clove garlic, crushed
salt and freshly ground
  black pepper
Garnish
lettuce leaves

Serves 4

Wipe the tomatoes and slice off the tops.
Scoop out the flesh, leaving a firm tomato
case. Purée the tomato flesh with all the
remaining ingredients, using the double-
bladed chopping knife.

Divide the filling between the
tomatoes, replace the lids and serve cold
on a bed of lettuce.

◙ Nutty chicken salad

50 g/2 oz salted peanuts
1 clove garlic, peeled
6 tablespoons salad oil
150 ml/¼ pint
  unsweetened apple
  juice
freshly ground black
  pepper
1 small lettuce, washed
450 g/1 lb cooked
  chicken, cut in pieces
Garnish
1 (56-g/2-oz) can
  anchovy fillets
50 g/2 oz stuffed olives

Serves 4

Illustrated on page 75

Reduce the peanuts to a fine powder,
using the double-bladed chopping knife.
Add the garlic and oil and continue to
mix until creamy. Add the apple juice
and season with freshly ground black
pepper. Mix thoroughly to form a smooth
dressing.

Line a serving dish with lettuce leaves.
Toss the chicken in the dressing in a
separate bowl, then pile into the serving
dish, pouring any remaining dressing on
top.

Garnish with anchovy fillets and stuffed
olives.

Sauces and dressings

This chapter contains a wide variety of basic and unusual recipes which may be used to enhance the flavour of and complement meat, fish, vegetable and pasta dishes, making simple foods into something special. There is nothing to compare with the flavour of freshly made sauces such as mint, apple and cranberry, which can be made in minutes. Espagnole, a sauce which can be used as a basis for making other classic sauces, is useful to make in bulk and freeze for use later.

Sauces can be made with complete confidence using the food processor, producing successful results every time.

◙ Basic mayonnaise

1 egg
1 teaspoon castor sugar
pinch of dry mustard
salt and freshly ground
   black pepper
300 ml/½ pint oil
1 teaspoon wine vinegar

Makes 300 ml/½ pint

Place the whole egg, sugar, mustard and seasoning in the bowl and mix for a few seconds using the double-bladed chopping knife. With the motor switched on, pour the oil through the feed tube in a slow trickle. The mayonnaise will thicken slowly. Mix in the vinegar at the end.

Variations

Avocado mayonnaise Peel an avocado and remove the stone. Add the flesh to the egg and seasonings and continue as above.

Garlic mayonnaise Add 1 crushed clove of garlic to the egg and seasonings and continue as above.

Green mayonnaise Leave the mayonnaise in the bowl and add a handful of washed watercress leaves. Using the double-bladed chopping knife, mix until the watercress is very finely chopped.

Cucumber mayonnaise Peel a quarter of a cucumber and place in the feed tube. Grate, using the grating disc. Drain well and stir into the prepared mayonnaise with a few chopped chives.

Tartare sauce Finely chop 2 gherkins, 1 spring onion and 2 tablespoons capers, using the double-bladed chopping knife. Stir into the prepared mayonnaise.

Nutty chicken salad (see page 72)

⬛ Remoulade sauce

First make the basic mayonnaise. Chop the remaining ingredients together, using the double-bladed chopping knife. Add the mayonnaise to the chopped ingredients and mix quickly for a few seconds until well combined.

Serve with cold meat, poultry and shellfish.

300 ml/½ pint basic mayonnaise (see page 74)
4 anchovy fillets
1 teaspoon French mustard
few sprigs parsley
1 teaspoon capers
1 gherkin
few sprigs fresh tarragon

Makes 300 ml/½ pint

⬛ Hollandaise sauce

Place the yolks and boiling water in the bowl and mix well, using the double-bladed chopping knife. Add the vinegar and lemon juice and mix again. Slowly pour the melted butter through the feed tube, with the motor running. Transfer the sauce to a small bowl and place over a saucepan of hot water. Stir continuously until thick. Serve immediately.

3 egg yolks
3 tablespoons boiling water
1 tablespoon wine vinegar
1 tablespoon lemon juice
100 g/4 oz butter, melted

Makes 150 ml/¼ pint

Italian sauce (see page 78)

◪ Espagnole sauce

2 rashers bacon, rinds removed
1 onion
1 stick of celery
2 small carrots
4 mushrooms
2 tablespoons oil
25 g/1 oz flour
450 ml/¾ pint stock
2 tablespoons tomato purée
salt and freshly ground black pepper
3 tablespoons chopped parsley
1 bay leaf

Makes 300 ml/½ pint

Roughly chop the bacon, onion, celery, carrots and mushrooms, using the double-bladed chopping knife. Heat the oil and sauté the vegetables until golden. Stir in the flour and cook for a few minutes until golden brown. Gradually stir in the stock and the remaining ingredients. Bring to the boil, cover and simmer for 45 minutes – 1 hour.

Remove the bay leaf and purée the sauce, using the double-bladed chopping knife, until smooth. If preferred, the sauce can be sieved before serving.

Serve with meat dishes.

◪ Italian sauce

Illustrated on page 76

few sprigs fresh basil or parsley
50 g/2 oz Parmesan cheese, broken into chunks
3–4 tablespoons peanut or olive oil
25 g/1 oz walnuts
1 clove garlic
salt and freshly ground black pepper

Makes about 100 g/4 oz

Finely chop the herbs and Parmesan, using the double-bladed chopping knife, until a paste is formed – about 1–2 minutes. Pour the oil slowly through the feed tube and mix until well combined. Add the nuts, garlic and seasoning and mix to a soft paste.

Use as a topping for soups or toss with hot cooked pasta.

🖫 Herb butter

Illustrated on page 2

Chop the herbs finely, using the double-bladed chopping knife. Mix the herbs, butter and seasoning together thoroughly, using the double-bladed chopping knife.

few sprigs of fresh
  herbs
100 g / 4 oz butter
salt and freshly ground
  black pepper

Makes 100 g / 4 oz

🖫 Bread sauce

Peel the onion and stud with the cloves. Place the milk in the saucepan with the onion. Bring to the boil and simmer gently for 10 minutes.

Remove the crusts and make the bread into breadcrumbs, using the double-bladed chopping knife.

Remove the onion from the milk, stir in the breadcrumbs and infuse for 30 minutes. Add the butter and reheat, stirring all the time. Season to taste.

1 onion
6 cloves
300 ml / ½ pint milk
2 slices white bread
25 g / 1 oz butter
salt and freshly ground
  black pepper

Makes 300 ml / ½ pint

🖫 Onion sauce

Peel the onions and slice thinly, using the slicing disc. Cook in boiling water for 10 minutes, then drain.

Place the flour, butter and milk in a saucepan and bring to the boil whisking all the time. Season and add the drained onions and cream. Serve with lamb.

2 onions
25 g / 1 oz flour
25 g / 1 oz butter
300 ml / ½ pint milk
salt and freshly ground
  black pepper
2 tablespoons cream

Makes 300 ml / ½ pint

◙ Fresh mint sauce

large bunch fresh mint
  leaves
2 tablespoons boiling
  water
2 tablespoons sugar
2–3 tablespoons wine
  vinegar

Makes about 150 ml/
  ¼ pint

Trim the mint, removing the stalks. Chop finely, using the double-bladed chopping knife. Place the chopped mint in a small basin and pour over the boiling water and sugar. Stir well and leave until cold. Add the vinegar and serve.

◙ Apple sauce

450 g/1 lb cooking
  apples
2–3 tablespoons water
sugar, to taste
15 g/½ oz butter

Makes 300 ml/½ pint

Peel, core and slice the apples and place in a saucepan with the water. Cook until the apple becomes soft. Allow to cool then mix to a purée with the sugar and butter, using the double-bladed chopping knife.

◙ Cranberry sauce

150 ml/¼ pint water
175 g/6 oz sugar
225 g/8 oz cranberries
lemon juice, to taste

Makes 300 ml/½ pint

Dissolve the sugar and water over a low heat. Bring to the boil and add the cranberries. Cover and simmer until the fruit is soft; 8–10 minutes. Cool and then mix to a purée, using the double-bladed chopping knife. Add lemon juice to taste.

⚙ Spicy tomato sauce

Peel and clean the vegetables and chop roughly with the bacon, using the double-bladed chopping knife. Melt the butter and oil and sauté the chopped vegetables. Stir in the flour and cook for 1 minute. Add the remaining ingredients and bring to the boil. Cover and simmer for 45 minutes.

Purée the sauce until smooth, using the double-bladed chopping knife. Adjust the seasoning if necessary.

1 onion
2 carrots
2 sticks celery
2 rashers bacon, rinds
   removed
25 g/1 oz butter
1 tablespoon oil
25 g/1 oz flour
1 (425-g/15-oz) can
   tomatoes
3 tablespoons tomato
   purée
$\frac{1}{4}$ teaspoon ground mace
freshly ground nutmeg
salt and freshly ground
   black pepper
few sprigs parsley
sprig fresh basil
150 ml/$\frac{1}{4}$ pint stock
sugar, to taste

Makes 300 ml/$\frac{1}{2}$ pint

⚙ French dressing

Mix all the ingredients together, using the double-bladed chopping knife, until an emulsion is formed. Keep in a screw-topped jar and shake well before using.

250 ml/8 fl oz oil
4$\frac{1}{2}$ tablespoons wine
   vinegar
1 teaspoon castor sugar
pinch of dry mustard
few sprigs parsley
salt and freshly ground
   black pepper

Makes 300 ml/$\frac{1}{2}$ pint

Watercress dressing

2 bunches watercress
150 ml/¼ pint double
 cream
salt and freshly ground
 black pepper
few drops lemon juice

Makes 150 ml/¼ pint

Trim the watercress, removing any
tough stems. Place in a saucepan with a
little water and bring to the boil. Simmer
for 5–8 minutes. Drain well and chop
finely, using the double-bladed
chopping knife.
   Bring the cream to the boil and stir in
the finely chopped watercress. Season to
taste and add a few drops of lemon juice.
Serve with salmon.

Roquefort dressing

175 g/6 oz cream
 cheese
75 g/3 oz Roquefort
 cheese
1 spring onion
few sprigs parsley
lemon juice, to taste
salt and freshly ground
 black pepper
pinch of cayenne
milk

*Makes about 300 ml/
 ½ pint*

Mix all the ingredients together until
smooth, using the double-bladed
chopping knife, adding sufficient milk to
mix.
   Serve with salads and cold meats.

Desserts

Sorbets, ice creams, flans, soufflés and cheesecakes can all be made quite effortlessly with the aid of a food processor, as it is such an excellent way to purée fruit really smoothly. Delightful and interesting flavours can be combined to provide a delicious end to any meal. Use the machine for all the pastry bases and for decorations too – nuts, chocolate or crystallised fruit can be quickly chopped or grated to add that special, last-minute touch.

🍎 🔪 Cheese apple flan

225 g/8 oz shortcrust
   pastry (see page 96)
2 tablespoons apricot
   jam
450 g/1 lb cooking
   apples, peeled, cored
   and quartered
50 g/2 oz soft brown
   sugar
75 g/3 oz Cheshire
   cheese
egg white for brushing
To serve
clotted cream

Serves 6 – 8

Roll out three-quarters of the pastry and use it to line a 23-cm/9-inch flan ring. Bake blind in a moderately hot oven (200°C, 400°F, Gas Mark 6) for 15 minutes. Spread the apricot jam over the base of the flan.

Slice the apples, using the slicing disc. Arrange the slices in the flan ring and sprinkle with the sugar.

Crumble the cheese into the bowl and chop finely, using the double-bladed chopping knife. Sprinkle over the flan.

Roll out the remaining pastry and cut into strips. Arrange the strips in a lattice pattern over the flan. Brush over with lightly beaten egg white. Bake in a moderately hot oven (200°C, 400°F, Gas Mark 6) for a further 20 – 30 minutes. Serve hot with clotted cream.

🔪 Baked raspberry cheesecake

75 g/3 oz butter
175 g/6 oz digestive
   biscuits
¼ teaspoon mixed spice
1 (227-g/8-oz) packet
   frozen raspberries,
   defrosted
450 g/1 lb cottage
   cheese
4 eggs
150 g/5 oz castor sugar
25 g/1 oz plain flour
Decoration
whipped cream

Serves 6 – 8

Melt the butter in a saucepan. Break the biscuits into the bowl and make into fine breadcrumbs, using the double-bladed chopping knife. Combine this with the melted butter and mixed spice. Use to line the base of a greased, loose-bottomed 20-cm/8-inch cake tin. Leave to chill.

Purée the defrosted raspberries using the double-bladed chopping knife. Remove from the bowl and set aside. Beat the cottage cheese, eggs, sugar and flour together until smooth, using the double-bladed chopping knife.

Turn this into a mixing bowl and stir in the fruit purée, mixing well. Pour this filling over the biscuit base and cook in a moderate oven (160°C, 325°F, Gas Mark 3) for 1¼ hours. Cool in the oven with the door open. Chill well and serve cold, decorated with freshly whipped cream.

🔟 Strawberry cheesecake

Roll out the pastry and use to line a 23-cm/9-inch fluted flan ring. Prick the base and bake blind in a moderately hot oven (200°C, 400°F, Gas Mark 6) for 15–20 minutes. Remove the paper lining and reduce the oven temperature to moderate (180°C, 350°F, Gas Mark 4) for a further 10–15 minutes. Leave to cool.

Purée the strawberries, using the double-bladed chopping knife. Add the cottage cheese, soured cream, egg yolks and sugar, and beat together.

Soften the gelatine in 3 tablespoons of warm water. Stir well in a basin over hot water until the gelatine has completely dissolved. Cool slightly, then pour into the strawberry mixture through the feed tube, mixing all the time with the double-bladed chopping knife.

Beat the egg whites until stiff, then fold carefully into the fruit and cheese mixture. Pour into the cooked flan case and chill until set. Decorate with whipped cream and halved strawberries.

225 g/8 oz sweet wholemeal pastry (see page 96)
225 g/8 oz fresh strawberries
225 g/8 oz cottage cheese
1 (142-ml/5-fl oz) carton soured cream
2 eggs, separated
75 g/3 oz castor sugar
15 g/½ oz gelatine
grated rind and juice of 1 lemon

Decoration
whipped cream
few strawberries, halved

Serves 6–8

◙ Lime splice

1 (200-g/7-oz) packet
  ginger nuts
50 g/2 oz butter, melted
grated rind and juice of
  1 lime
lime cordial
2 teaspoons cornflour
50 g/2 oz castor sugar
1 egg, separated
175 ml/6 fl oz double
  cream
Decoration
slices of lime
whipped cream

Serves 6–8

Illustrated on page 93

Roughly break up the ginger nuts and make into fine crumbs, using the double-bladed chopping knife. Pour the melted butter through the feed tube and mix for a few seconds. Use the mixture to line the base and sides of a 20-cm/8-inch flan dish. Press the crumbs down firmly and leave to chill.

Make up the juice of the lime to 75 ml/ 3 fl oz with lime cordial. Then make the mixture up to 150 ml/¼ pint with water.

Pour a little onto the cornflour and mix well. Heat the remaining juice. When hot pour onto the cornflour mixture, mix well and return to the heat to thicken. Add the grated lime rind and sugar. Allow to cool slightly then beat in the egg yolk. When the mixture is completely cold, whisk the egg white and fold into the mixture with a metal spoon. Lightly whip the cream and fold it into the mixture. Pour into the chilled biscuit case and decorate with slices of lime and whipped cream.

◙ Tipsy gala ring

Illustrated on the jacket

Put the water and butter in a saucepan. When the butter has melted, bring quickly to the boil. Remove from the heat and beat in the flour. Continue to cook until the mixture comes away from the side of the pan. Allow to cool then turn the mixture into the bowl, fitted with the double-bladed chopping knife. Gradually add the beaten eggs through the feed tube, mixing all the time. Use the mixture to fill a piping bag, fitted with a plain 2.5-cm/1-inch nozzle, and pipe a 23-cm/9-inch ring onto a greased baking tray. Sprinkle the top with the almonds and a little sugar. Bake in a moderately hot oven (200°C, 400°F, Gas Mark 6) for 20 minutes. Reduce the temperature to moderate (180°C, 350°F, Gas Mark 4) for a further 20–25 minutes. Remove from the oven and cool.

For the filling, whip the cream and Cointreau together. Peel and chop the peaches and fold into the cream with the orange rind. Split the choux ring and fill with the cream mixture. Dust the top with icing sugar.

150 ml/¼ pint water
50 g/2 oz butter
65 g/2½ oz plain flour, sieved
2 eggs, beaten
25 g/1 oz flaked almonds
castor sugar to sprinkle

Filling
300 ml/½ pint double cream
3 tablespoons Cointreau
3 fresh peaches
grated rind of ½ orange

Decoration
icing sugar

Serves 6

◘ ◖ Apple and almond puff

1 (212-g/7½-oz) packet
  puff pastry
100 g/4 oz dried
  apricots, soaked
  overnight
450 g/1 lb cooking
  apples, peeled, cored
  and quartered
40 g/1½ oz brown sugar
¼ teaspoon ground
  cloves
grated rind of ½ lemon
lightly beaten egg for
  brushing
castor sugar to sprinkle
Almond paste
100 g/4 oz ground
  almonds
50 g/2 oz castor sugar
50 g/2 oz icing sugar
½ teaspoon lemon juice
½ egg, lightly beaten
To serve
clotted cream

Serves 6–8

Roll the pastry to an oblong 25 x 30 cm/ 10 x 12 inches, and place on a dampened baking tray.

To make the almond paste, mix all the ingredients together, using the double-bladed chopping knife. Turn out onto a board, lightly dusted with icing sugar, and knead lightly. Roll out to an oblong 2.5 cm/1 inch smaller than the pastry and lay it on top. Set aside and leave to chill.

Chop the apricots roughly, using the double-bladed chopping knife. Slice the apples, using the slicing disc by placing a few quarters at a time in the feed tube and pressing down lightly with the plastic pusher. Mix the apricots, apple, brown sugar, ground cloves and grated lemon rind in a mixing bowl and arrange this filling down the centre of the pastry. Bring each side of the pastry to the centre of the filling. Overlap the edges of the pastry and seal them together with water.

Turn the roll over so that the seam is underneath. Close each end of the pastry roll and fold them underneath. Decorate with any remaining pastry trimmings. Brush with beaten egg and sprinkle with castor sugar. Bake in a moderately hot oven (200°C, 400°F, Gas Mark 6) for 35 minutes. Serve hot or cold, with clotted cream.

Blinis with strawberries

Sprinkle the yeast onto the water and leave in a warm place until frothy.

Place the flours in the bowl and pour in the yeast liquid and warm milk through the feed tube. Mix together, using the double-bladed chopping knife, to form a smooth batter. Pour the batter into a clean basin, cover and leave in a warm place to rise for 1 – 1½ hours. Return the batter to the bowl and add the egg yolks, sugar and melted butter. Mix well and pour back into the basin. Cover and leave to rise again for 1 hour. Beat the mixture with a wooden spoon to knock the air out.

Melt a little butter in a frying pan and pour a little of the batter into the pan, tilting it so that the batter forms a circle about 13 cm/5 inches in diameter. When bubbles appear on the surface, turn and cook the other side. If the mixture is a little stiff, add some water to the batter. Serve the blinis hot, filled with soured cream and fresh strawberries.

Note Blinis are equally delicious served as a savoury, topped with crisp fried bacon, cream cheese or smoked cod's roe.

15 g/½ oz dried yeast
75 ml/3 fl oz warm water
75 g/3 oz plain
  wholemeal flour
225 g/8 oz plain flour
450 ml/¾ pint warm milk
2 egg yolks
1 teaspoon castor sugar
25 g/1 oz butter, melted
Filling
soured cream
fresh strawberries

Serves 6

◙ Spiced coffee soufflé

25 g/1 oz butter
25 g/1 oz plain flour
150 ml/¼ pint milk
50 g/2 oz castor sugar
4 eggs, separated
¼ teaspoon mixed spice
2 tablespoons instant
coffee

Serves 4

Place the butter, flour and milk in the bowl and mix until smooth, using the double-bladed chopping knife. Transfer to a saucepan and bring to the boil, stirring continuously. Cook until thick. Stir in the sugar and cook for a further 2 minutes.

Return the sauce to the bowl and add the egg yolks, mixed spice and coffee, dissolved in 2 teaspoons of hot water, Mix until smooth, using the double-bladed chopping knife.

Meanwhile whisk the egg whites until stiff. Add half the egg whites to the sauce in the bowl and mix them in well, using the double-bladed chopping knife. Transfer the mixture to a mixing bowl and fold in the remaining egg whites with a metal spoon.

Pour the soufflé mixture into a greased 1.25-litre/2-pint soufflé dish and bake in a moderately hot oven (190°C, 375°F, Gas Mark 5) for 35–40 minutes. Serve at once.

◙ Peach ice cream

450 ml/¾ pint milk
175 g/6 oz castor sugar
2 eggs
300 ml/½ pint double
cream
6 peaches

Serves 6

Illustrated on page 93

Whisk the milk, sugar and eggs together in a mixing bowl until well combined. Stand the bowl over a saucepan of hot water and cook until slightly thickened, stirring occasionally. Allow to cool.

Stir in the double cream and pour into a shallow freezer container. Partially freeze until slushy.

Skin the peaches, remove the stones and mix to a purée, using the double-bladed chopping knife. Add the partially frozen mixture and mix well. Return to the freezer until partially frozen. Using the double-bladed chopping knife, mix the ice cream until smooth and light in colour. Return the ice cream to the freezer and freeze until solid. Remove from the freezer and place in the refrigerator 1 hour before serving. Serve with fresh peaches.

▧ Gooseberry ice cream

Cook the gooseberries in their juice with 50 g/2 oz of the sugar until just tender. Mix to a fine purée, using the double-bladed chopping knife and cool.

Put the egg yolks and two of the whites into the bowl. Add the rest of the sugar and 250 ml/8 fl oz of the cream. Mix well, using the double-bladed chopping knife. Transfer to a mixing bowl and place over a pan of gently simmering water. Stir until the custard coats the back of the spoon and cool.

Whip the remaining cream lightly and whisk the egg white until stiff. Mix the fruit and lemon rind into the cooled custard. Fold in the cream and egg white with a metal spoon. Turn into a freezing container and freeze until hard. Allow to soften in the refrigerator for 1 – 2 hours before serving.

450 g/1 lb frozen goose-
  berries, defrosted
100 g/4 oz castor sugar
3 eggs, separated
300 ml/½ pint double
  cream
grated rind of ½ lemon

Serves 6 – 8

🍋 Plum and ginger sorbet

450 g / 1 lb firm yellow
  plums
100 g / 4 oz castor sugar
25 g / 1 oz crystallised
  ginger, chopped
4 egg whites
Decoration
whipped cream
chopped nuts

Serves 4

Skin and stone the plums. Purée them, using the double-bladed chopping knife. Transfer the purée to a bowl and stir in the sugar and ginger. Freeze this mixture until it is just firm.

Whisk the egg whites until stiff. Mash the plum and ginger mixture to break down the ice crystals. Fold in the egg whites and refreeze. Remove the sorbet from the freezer 30 minutes before it is required. Serve in glasses, decorated with whipped cream and chopped nuts.

🍋 Coeur à l'orange

225 g / 8 oz cottage
  cheese
300 ml / ½ pint double
  cream
4 tablespoons fresh
  orange juice
50 g / 2 oz castor sugar
2 egg whites
Decoration
slices of orange
mint leaves, optional

Serves 8

Illustrated opposite and on the jacket
Mash the cottage cheese, using the double-bladed chopping knife, until really smooth. Lightly whip the cream and orange juice together until soft but not stiff. Add to the cheese with the sugar and mix until well combined. Whisk the egg whites until stiff and fold into the cream mixture with a metal spoon. Divide the mixture between 8 special heart-shaped moulds with holes in the base for draining or 8 individual ramekin dishes with a piece of muslin tied over each, turned upside down. Allow to drain overnight before serving. Either serve in the moulds or turn out and decorate with slices of orange and mint leaves.

*Peach ice cream (see page 90); Coeur à l'orange
(see above); Lime splice (see page 86)*

Baking

Whether you are making feather-light cakes and pastries, bread doughs or a simple butter icing, the food processor can beat, knead or cream for you in seconds. Extreme care must be taken not to overmix, so keep stopping the machine at regular intervals to check. *The type A* machine has a plastic blade which is suitable for mixtures requiring minimal mixing. Otherwise use the double-bladed chopping knife or the chopper/blender. Always remember to check the capacity of the bowl or container before beginning a recipe.

Granary loaf (see page 98); Devil's food cake (see page 101); Wholemeal drop scones (see page 98)

Shortcrust pastry

225 g/8 oz plain flour
100 g/4 oz margarine or
  butter, cut into cubes
2–3 tablespoons water

Makes 225 g/8 oz

Using the double-bladed chopping knife, mix the flour and margarine together until the mixture resembles fine breadcrumbs. Add the water through the feed tube and mix to form a dough. Knead lightly on a floured board and use as required.

Variations
 Cheese pastry Grate 50 g/2 oz cheese, using the grating disc, and add to the flour with a pinch of mustard and cayenne.

Wholemeal pastry Substitute plain wholemeal flour for the white flour.

Sweet wholemeal pastry Add 25 g/1 oz castor sugar to the above recipe.

Basic choux pastry

50 g/2 oz butter
150 ml/¼ pint water
70 g/2½ oz plain flour,
  sieved
2 eggs

Makes 150 ml/¼ pint

Place the butter and water in a saucepan and heat gently until the butter has melted. Bring quickly to the boil, remove from the heat and beat in the flour. Return to the heat and cook, stirring all the time for a minute. Allow to cool.

Beat the eggs lightly. Place the cooled mixture in the bowl and, using the double-bladed chopping knife, gradually pour in the beaten eggs, a little at a time. Mix to a stiffish paste. Use as required.

Variation
 Cheese choux pastry Grate 25 g/1 oz cheese, using the grating disc and add before mixing in the eggs.

◨ Hot water crust pastry

Heat the margarine and water together in a saucepan until the margarine has melted, then bring rapidly to the boil. Place the remaining ingredients in the bowl and pour the hot liquid through the feed tube. Mix to a dough, using the double-bladed chopping knife. Turn out onto a floured board and knead lightly until smooth. Leave to rest in a polythene bag for 30 minutes. Use as required.

75 g/3 oz margarine
150 ml/¼ pint water
175 g/10 oz plain flour
½ teaspoon salt
1 egg yolk

Makes 275 g/10 oz

◨ ◧ Cheese and onion rolls

Illustrated on the jacket

Peel and quarter the onion, and chop finely, using the double-bladed chopping knife. Sauté the onion in the butter until soft. Grate the cheese, using the grating disc. Sprinkle the dried yeast onto the milk and leave in a warm place until frothy.

Place the flour and seasonings in the bowl with the cooked onion and grated cheese. Pour the yeast mixture through the feed tube and mix, using the double-bladed chopping knife, to form a dough. Cover and leave in a warm place until double in size – about 1 hour. Turn onto a floured board and knead lightly.

Divide into 8 portions and shape into long rolls. Place side by side in a greased 1-kg/2-lb loaf tin, so that the rolls touch each other. Cover and leave to rise in a warm place for 30 minutes. Brush with beaten egg, then bake in a moderately hot oven (200°C, 400°F, Gas Mark 6) for 20 – 25 minutes.

1 small onion
15 g/½ oz butter
50 g/2 oz cheese
3 teaspoons dried yeast
150 ml/¼ pint milk
225 g/8 oz plain flour
pinch of salt
1 teaspoon dry mustard
beaten egg to glaze

Makes 8 rolls

Granary loaf

¾ teaspoon dried yeast
150 ml/¼ pint warm
water
½ teaspoon castor sugar
100 g/4 oz granary
bread meal
100 g/4 oz plain
wholemeal flour
pinch of salt
15 g/½ oz butter
cracked wheat

Makes 1 loaf

Illustrated on page 94

Sprinkle the yeast onto the warm water and stir in the sugar. Leave in a warm place until frothy.

Place the flours, salt and butter in the bowl, and mix for a few seconds, using the double-bladed chopping knife. Pour the yeast liquid through the feed tube and mix to form a dough. Turn onto a floured board and knead for a minute. Cover and leave in a warm place to rise until doubled in size – about 1 hour. Knead again and shape into a round. Place on a greased baking tray and cut a cross on top of the dough. Cover and prove for 30 minutes in a warm place. Brush with a little salt water and sprinkle with cracked wheat. Bake in a hot oven (220°C, 425°F, Gas Mark 7) for 20–30 minutes.

Wholemeal drop scones

175 g/6 oz strong plain
flour
175 g/6 oz plain
wholemeal flour
15 g/½ oz fresh yeast
300 ml/½ pint warm
water
200 ml/7 fl oz milk
¼ teaspoon salt
½ teaspoon bicarbonate
of soda

Makes about 30

Illustrated on page 94

Mix the flours and pour half into a separate mixing bowl. Mix the yeast with the water until well combined. Pour into the centre of flour and leave until frothy.

Place in the bowl and gradually mix in the remaining flour, using the double-bladed chopping knife. Pour the milk onto the dough through the feed tube and mix until the batter is smooth. Lastly, add the salt and bicarbonate of soda. Place spoonfuls of the yeast batter on a greased griddle or frying pan and cook over a low heat. When bubbles appear on the surface turn over and cook on the other side. Serve hot with butter.

◙ Almond shortbread

Mix the flour, rice flour, ground almonds and butter together, using the double-bladed chopping knife, until the mixture resembles fine breadcrumbs. Add the remaining ingredients and mix into a dough. Place in an 18-cm/7-inch square shallow tin, pressing down until smooth. Prick all over with a fork. Bake in a moderate oven (180°C, 350°F Gas Mark 4) for 50–60 minutes. Mark into fingers while hot and sprinkle with sugar.

100 g/4 oz plain flour
50 g/2 oz rice flour
50 g/2 oz ground almonds
100 g/4 oz butter
75 g/3 oz sugar
1 egg yolk
2 tablespoons milk
few drops of almond essence
castor sugar to sprinkle

Makes 14 fingers

◙ Peach and orange teabread

Illustrated on the jacket
Drain the peaches and chop with the cherries, using the double-bladed chopping knife. Simmer the chopped fruit in the orange juice for 5 minutes.

Using the double-bladed chopping knife, mix the butter into the flour. Add the remaining ingredients and mix well. Place in a greased 1-kg/2-lb loaf tin. Bake in a moderate oven (180°C, 350°F, Gas Mark 4) for 1–1¼ hours.

Slice and spread with butter.

100 g/4 oz dried peaches, soaked overnight
100 g/4 oz glacé cherries
grated rind and juice of 2 small oranges
50 g/2 oz butter
225 g/8 oz self-raising flour
75 g/3 oz soft brown sugar
100 g/4 oz raisins
2 eggs
1–2 tablespoons milk

Makes 1 (1-kg/2-lb) loaf

Cherry gâteau

175 g/6 oz butter
175 g/6 oz castor sugar
3 eggs
165 g/5½ oz self-raising
  flour
15 g/½ oz cocoa powder,
  sieved

Filling
1 (142-ml/5-fl oz) carton
  black cherry yogurt
1 (425-g/15-oz) can
  black cherries,
  drained
150 ml/¼ pint double
  cream

Serves 6 – 8

Cream the butter and sugar together until light and fluffy, using the double-bladed chopping knife. Add the eggs one at a time, adding a little of the flour with each egg after the first. Mix well between each addition. Add the remaining flour and cocoa and mix for a few seconds only. If the flour has not been completely incorporated, use a spatula to fold it in. Grease and base line two (20-cm/8-inch) sandwich tins. Bake in the centre of a moderate oven (160°C, 325°F, Gas Mark 3) for 30 – 40 minutes.

Turn out and cool on a wire tray. When cool, sandwich the cakes together with the yogurt and half the canned cherries. Whip the cream and spread a little over the top of the gâteau. Pipe the remaining cream around the edge and fill the centre with the remaining cherries.

Note If liked the gâteau can be sprinkled with some of the canned cherry juice before assembling.

⑤ Florentines

Using the double-bladed chopping knife, finely chop the walnuts, raisins and glacé cherries.

Melt the sugar, syrup and butter together, remove from the heat and add all the remaining ingredients except the chocolate. Place teaspoonfuls of the mixture well apart on greased baking trays. Bake in a moderate oven (180°C, 350°F, Gas Mark 4) for 8–10 minutes. Remove carefully with a palette knife and allow to cool.

Spread one side of each florentine with melted chocolate and mark a design on each, using a fork.

25 g / 1 oz walnuts
25 g / 1 oz raisins
50 g / 2 oz glacé cherries
50 g / 2 oz demerara sugar
1 tablespoon golden syrup
50 g / 2 oz butter
40 g / 1½ oz plain flour
25 g / 1 oz mixed cut peel
75 g / 3 oz chocolate, melted

Makes 18

⑤ Devil's food cake

Illustrated on page 94

Place the margarine, syrup and dry ingredients in the bowl and mix, using the double-bladed chopping knife, until the fat is incorporated. Beat the milk and eggs together and pour through the feed tube with the machine switched on, mixing until well combined. Pour the mixture into two greased and lined 20-cm/ 8-inch sandwich tins. Bake in a cool oven (150°C, 300°F, Gas Mark 2) for 50–55 minutes. Turn out and cool on a wire rack.

For the icing, mix together the cocoa and hot water, then combine all the ingredients, using the double-bladed chopping knife. Use the icing to sandwich the two layers together and to spread over the top and sides of the cake. Press flaked almonds around the sides.

175 g / 6 oz soft margarine
175 g / 6 oz golden syrup
175 g / 6 oz castor sugar
50 g / 2 oz ground almonds
175 g / 6 oz plain flour
50 g / 2 oz cocoa
175 ml / 6 fl oz milk
2 eggs
Icing
1 tablespoon cocoa
2 tablespoons hot water
75 g / 3 oz butter
225 g / 8 oz icing sugar
100 g / 4 oz flaked almonds, toasted

Makes 12 slices

Raspberry japonais meringue

100 g/4 oz left-over
  sponge cake
50 g/2 oz cornflour
150 g/5 oz castor sugar
3 egg whites
few drops of almond
  essence
Filling
225 g/8 oz
  raspberries
150 ml/¼ pint double
  cream, whipped

Serves 6

Make the cake into fine crumbs, using the double-bladed chopping knife. Mix together with the cornflour and sugar.

Whisk the egg whites until stiff, then fold in the crumb mixture. Line 2 baking sheets with parchment paper and pipe the meringue, using a large plain nozzle, into two 20-cm/8-inch circles. Bake in a moderate oven (160°C, 325°F, Gas Mark 3) for 30–40 minutes until crisp and golden. When cold, remove the meringues from the parchment.

Sandwich the meringue together with some of the raspberries mixed with a little of the whipped cream. Use the remainder to decorate the top of the meringue.

Toddlers' Food

Feeding babies and young children is often a problem, especially for first-time mums! One answer is to make your own foods using the food processor. Small portions of the family's meal can be puréed or chopped, but always use fresh food and make sure that all equipment is perfectly clean. Use up any left-over food within 24 hours, remember too, that if you own a freezer, individual portions can be frozen. Do not add too much seasoning to baby foods; the amount of sugar should be limited too.

◉ Vegetable purées

50 g/2 oz cooked root
  vegetable, e.g.
  carrots, parsnips,
  swedes
2 tablespoons milk or
  stock
or
50 g/2 oz cooked
  green vegetable,
  e.g. spinach,
  cabbage, beans,
  broccoli
1 tablespoon milk or
  stock

Serves 1

Roughly chop the cooked vegetables
and purée in the bowl with 1 or 2
tablespoons of liquid, using the double-
bladed chopping-knife. Reheat gently in
a small saucepan if necessary.

◉ Liver and bacon purée

50 g/2 oz cooked lamb's
  liver
1 rasher lean bacon,
  lightly grilled
2 teaspoons tomato
  ketchup
6 tablespoons milk or
  milk and stock

Serves 1

Finely chop the liver and bacon, using
the double-bladed chopping knife. Add
the other ingredients and mix to a broth
using the double-bladed chopping knife.
Pour into a small saucepan and heat
gently. Serve warm.

Tasty toppers

A crisp slice of toast is an ideal base for savoury and sweet spreads. More substantial mixtures can also be used, making a quick and easy snack meal. Try some of the following toppers and spreads.

🔿 🌰 Ham and cheese savoury

Chop the ham finely, using the double bladed chopping knife. Grate the cheese, using the grating disc. Make the sauce by combining the flour, butter and milk, using the double-bladed chopping knife, until smooth. Pour this into a pan and bring to the boil gently, stirring all the time, until thick. Season lightly if the dish is for a child over 9 months old. Stir in the chopped ham and 50 g/2 oz of the grated cheese.

Toast the bread under the grill on one side, then spread the savoury mixture over the untoasted side. Sprinkle with the remaining cheese and grill until golden brown. Serve immediately.

1 slice cooked ham
75 g/3 oz Cheddar
  cheese
15 g/½ oz flour
15 g/½ oz butter
150 ml/¼ pint milk
2 slices bread

Serves 2

🔿 Banana cheese delight

Purée the banana, using the double-bladed chopping knife. Add the cottage cheese and ground cinnamon and purée again.

Toast the bread on one side. Butter the other side and spread with the topping. Sprinkle with demerara sugar and grill until the sugar melts. Serve warm.

1 ripe banana
1 (113-g/4-oz) carton
  cottage cheese
pinch of ground
  cinnamon
2 slices bread
butter for spreading
2 tablespoons demerara
  sugar

Serves 2

◙ Egg spread

2 eggs, hard-boiled
25 g/1 oz butter
salt (optional)

Makes 100 g/4 oz

Shell the eggs and place in the bowl. Chop finely, using the double-bladed chopping knife. Add the butter and mix well. Season the spread if it is to be used for older children, but this spread is ideal served unseasoned on rusks for babies over 9 months old.

◙ ◙ Cheddar cheese spread

100 g/4 oz Cheddar
    cheese
50 g/2 oz butter
salt and freshly ground
    black pepper
pinch of dry mustard

Makes 175 g/6 oz

Grate the cheese finely, using the grating disc. Place in the bowl with the butter, seasonings and mustard and mix thoroughly, using the double-bladed chopping knife. Store in the refrigerator.

Variations
Add one of the following to the basic cheese spread mixture:

25 g/1 oz chopped nuts
1 tablespoon mango chutney
1 hard-boiled egg, finely chopped
1 tablespoon chopped parsley
½ teaspoon curry paste

◙ Fruit purées

Puréed fruit is easily digested by babies over 6 months old, and is a versatile ingredient in many recipes. Try stirring puréed fruit into custard, natural yogurt, or cottage cheese, and use it as a topping for ice cream. Quantities to use will vary from baby to baby, so use the quantity suggested as a rough guide.

To prepare the fruit for puréeing, it should be made reasonably soft and not too sweet. Soft fruits such as bananas, peaches, plums and melons only need peeling. Hard fruits like apples and dessert pears, and sharp-tasting fruits such as blackcurrants and gooseberries, should be stewed with a little sugar and water until soft. Dried fruits, sultanas, dried apricots and prunes, should be soaked overnight, then brought to the boil and simmered for 15 – 20 minutes.

    Place the prepared fruit in the bowl and purée, using the double-bladed chopping knife.

50 g/2 oz fruit

Serves 1

◙ Jelly snow

Dissolve the jelly cubes in the boiling water. Add the evaporated milk and leave in a basin to set. Whisk the egg white until stiff.

    Turn the set jelly into the bowl and mix until frothy, using the double-bladed chopping knife. Fold in the egg white with a metal spoon and divide the mixture between 2 glasses. Leave to set.

½ (600-ml/1-pint) strawberry or raspberry jelly block
150 ml/¼ pint boiling water
150 ml/¼ pint evaporated milk
1 egg white

Serves 2

🌀 Gingerbread shapes

100 g/4 oz soft brown
  sugar
100 g/4 oz black treacle
1 teaspoon ground
  ginger
1 teaspoon mixed spice
1 teaspoon baking
  powder
75 g/3 oz butter
350 g/12 oz plain flour
pinch of salt
1 egg
Decoration
glacé icing
currants

Makes 15 – 20

Place the sugar, treacle and spices in a saucepan and heat gently until the sugar has melted. Bring quickly to the boil, then remove from the heat and beat in the baking powder.

Cream the butter, using the double-bladed chopping knife. Pour the treacle mixture through the feed tube and mix until smooth. Then add half the flour, the salt and egg. Combine well, using the double-bladed chopping knife. Add the remaining flour and mix to a smooth dough. Turn onto a lightly floured board and knead gently until smooth. Place the dough in the refrigerator for 30 minutes.

Roll out the dough to 3 mm/⅛ inch in thickness and cut out shapes, for example men or animals, using metal cutters. Place on floured baking trays and bake in a moderate oven (160°C, 325°F, Gas Mark 3) for 8 – 10 minutes. Carefully lift the gingerbread off the trays, and leave to cool on wire racks. Decorate with piped glacé icing and currants.

Healthy eating

Today many people are aware of the benefits to their health derived from eating less refined foods such as wholemeal flours and pasta, brown sugar, pulses and nuts. In this chapter you will find a selection of delicious sweet and savoury recipes, using health foods. The food processor chops nuts and fruit effortlessly and prepares rubbed-in mixtures, cakes and batters in a fraction of the time it usually takes. All the foods used in this chapter are obtainable from health-food stores and larger supermarkets.

◙ Spiced oaties

175 g/6 oz plain flour
75 g/3 oz butter
50 g/2 oz medium
  oatmeal
50 g/2 oz chopped
  mixed nuts
25 g/1 oz demerara sugar
¼ teaspoon allspice
4 tablespoons milk
1 egg yolk
demerara sugar to
  sprinkle

Makes 14 – 16

Illustrated opposite

Mix the flour and butter, using the double-bladed chopping knife, until the mixture resembles fine breadcrumbs. Transfer to a mixing bowl and stir in the oatmeal, nuts, sugar and allspice. Mix the milk and egg yolk and make a well in the centre of the flour mixture. Stir in the liquid gradually to form a biscuit dough. Knead lightly on a floured surface until smooth. Roll out to 3 mm/⅛ inch in thickness and cut out rounds with a 6-cm/2½-inch fluted cutter. Arrange on greased baking trays and bake in a moderately hot oven (200°C, 400°F, Gas Mark 6) for 10 – 15 minutes. Sprinkle the biscuits with sugar while hot and leave to cool on racks.

◙ Peanut butter spread

100 g/4 oz salted
  peanuts
50 g/2 oz butter
salt

Makes 175 g/6 oz

Illustrated opposite

Finely chop the peanuts, using the double-bladed chopping knife. Add the butter and mix to form a smooth paste, using the double-bladed chopping knife. Add salt to taste.

Store in the refrigerator and use as required.

Spiced oaties (see above); Peanut butter spread (see above)

⬛ Buckwheat pancakes

Place the flours and salt in the bowl. Mix together the egg and milk and pour onto the flour. Mix to a smooth batter, using the double-bladed chopping knife. Use the batter to make 10–12 pancakes. Fry each to a light golden colour on both sides and keep hot.

Make a white sauce for the filling by mixing together the flour, butter and milk until smooth, using the double-bladed chopping knife. Bring this to the boil gradually, stirring continuously. Stir the tarragon and grated nutmeg into the sauce. Cut the bacon into pieces, then chop finely, using the double-bladed chopping knife. Fry gently in its own fat.

Meanwhile wash and trim the mushrooms and chop, using the double-bladed chopping knife. Add to the bacon and fry gently until tender. Mix the mushrooms and bacon into the sauce and reheat.

Spread the filling over each pancake and roll up. Arrange in an ovenproof dish and reheat in a moderate oven (180°C, 350°F, Gas Mark 4) for 10–15 minutes. Serve hot.

Batter
100 g / 4 oz buckwheat
 flour
50 g / 2 oz plain flour
½ teaspoon salt
1 egg, beaten
450 ml / ¾ pint milk

Filling
50 g / 2 oz flour
50 g / 2 oz butter
450 ml / ¾ pint milk
1 teaspoon chopped
 fresh tarragon
freshly grated nutmeg
100 g / 4 oz streaky
 bacon
100 g / 4 oz mushrooms

Makes 10–12

Beetroot chutney (see page 122); Pepper and onion pickle (see page 121)

Savoury nut loaf

225 g/8 oz mixed nuts
1 small onion
1 stick of celery
50 g/2 oz mushrooms
575 g/1¼ lb potatoes,
  cooked and mashed
1 teaspoon mixed herbs
¼ teaspoon freshly
  grated nutmeg
½ teaspoon sesame
  seeds
1 tablespoon tomato
  purée
salt and freshly ground
  black pepper
1 egg, beaten
sesame seeds to
  sprinkle

Serves 4

Finely chop the nuts, using the double-bladed chopping knife. Remove from the bowl. Peel and quarter the onion and cut the celery into 2.5-cm/1-inch pieces. Chop finely together, using the double-bladed chopping knife. Wipe and trim the mushrooms and chop finely, using the double-bladed chopping knife.

Mix the nuts, onion, celery and mushrooms together in a mixing bowl and work in the mashed potato, mixed herbs, nutmeg, sesame seeds, tomato purée and seasonings. Bind with the beaten egg and turn the mixture into a greased and lined 0.5-kg/1-lb loaf tin. Sprinkle the top with sesame seeds. Bake in a moderately hot oven (190°C, 375°F, Gas Mark 5) for 1 – 1¼ hours. Allow to cool in the tin, then turn out and cut into slices. Serve with a salad.

Health salad

50 g/2 oz mixed nuts
1 green pepper
1 large apple
2 carrots
1 stick of celery
1 banana
50 g/2 oz sultanas
25 g/1 oz sunflower
  seeds
2 tablespoons lemon
  juice
Garnish
chopped parsley

Serves 4

Roughly chop the nuts, using the double-bladed chopping knife. Remove and set aside in a large mixing bowl.

Quarter the green pepper, remove the seeds and cut into pieces. Peel and core the apple and cut into pieces. Finely chop the pepper and apple together, using the double-bladed chopping knife, and add to the nuts.

Scrape the carrots and grate, using the grating disc. Add to the nut mixture. Slice the celery and banana, using the slicing disc, and add to the mixture with the sultanas, sunflower seeds, and lemon juice. Garnish and serve immediately.

114

◑ ◐ Wholemeal pasta salad

Cook the macaroni in plenty of boiling salted water until tender – about 10 – 12 minutes. Drain and toss in a little oil to prevent sticking. Leave to cool.

Chop the hard-boiled eggs, using the double-bladed chopping knife, and stir into the mayonnaise. Finely slice the celery, using the slicing disc, and add to the mayonnaise mixture. Add the prawns, chopped parsley and lemon rind and mix well. Season and add celery salt, garlic salt, turmeric and paprika to taste. Stir in the cooked macaroni. Serve the salad slightly chilled, garnished with chopped parsley.

225 g/8 oz wholemeal
   macaroni
2 eggs, hard-boiled
150 ml/$\frac{1}{4}$ pint basic
   mayonnaise (see
   page 74)
1 stick of celery
225 g/8 oz frozen
   prawns, defrosted
2 tablespoons chopped
   parsley
grated rind of 1 lemon
salt and freshly ground
   black pepper
celery salt
garlic salt
turmeric
paprika
Garnish
chopped parsley

Serves 4 – 6

◨ ◪ Brown rice risotto

1 medium onion
1 red and green pepper
6 rashers bacon
3 tablespoons oil
100 g/4 oz mushrooms
225 g/8 oz brown rice
1 litre/1¾ pints stock
salt and freshly ground
   black pepper
75 g/3 oz Cheddar
   cheese
Garnish
chopped parsley

Serves 4

Peel and quarter the onion and chop, using the double-bladed chopping knife. Halve the pepper and remove the seeds. Cut into chunks and chop, using the double-bladed chopping knife. Remove from the bowl. Cut the bacon rashers into several pieces and chop, using the double-bladed chopping knife.

Fry the onion, pepper and bacon in the oil. Meanwhile wipe and trim the mushrooms. Chop, using the double-bladed chopping knife, and add to the onion mixture with the rice. Continue to fry gently for 2–3 minutes, then add the stock and seasonings.

Bring to the boil and simmer gently for 1–1¼ hours, stirring occasionally and adding more stock to moisten if necessary.

Grate the cheese, using the grating disc. Sprinkle the cheese over the risotto with some freshly chopped parsley, and serve hot.

◙ Brown bread ice cream

Make the bread into crumbs, using the double-bladed chopping knife. Spread the crumbs on a baking tray and place in a moderate oven (160°C, 325°F, Gas Mark 3) until crisp and lightly browned – about 15 minutes. Leave to cool.

Put the cream, sugar, egg yolks, rum (if used) and grated lemon rind in the bowl and mix until smooth, using the double-bladed chopping knife. Fold the breadcrumbs into the cream mixture. Beat the egg whites until stiff and fold into the mixture with a metal spoon.

Partially freeze the ice cream, then mix until smooth and light in colour, using the double-bladed chopping knife. Return to the freezer and freeze until solid. One hour before serving, remove from the freezer and place in the refrigerator.

4 slices brown bread (to make 100 g/4 oz crumbs)
450 ml/¾ pint double cream
75 g/3 oz soft dark brown sugar
2 eggs, separated
1 tablespoon rum (optional)
grated rind of ½ lemon

Serves 6

◙ Autumn crumble

Skin and stone the plums. Place in a greased 1.25-litre/2-pint ovenproof dish and sprinkle with the sugar.

Mix together the flours and butter, using the double-bladed chopping knife, until the mixture resembles fine breadcrumbs. Remove from the bowl and stir in the sugar and ground almonds. Spread the mixture over the plums and sprinkle with the flaked almonds. Bake in a moderately hot oven (190°C, 375°F, Gas Mark 5) for 45–50 minutes. Serve hot.

675 g/1½ lb ripe plums
50 g/2 oz sugar
Crumble topping
100 g/4 oz plain flour
100 g/4 oz rye flour
175 g/6 oz butter
100 g/4 oz brown sugar
50 g/2 oz ground almonds
50 g/2 oz flaked almonds

Serves 4–6

◙ Nectar cake

225 g/8 oz softened
  butter or margarine
100 g/4 oz soft brown
  sugar
100 g/4 oz castor sugar
4 eggs
100 g/4 oz heather
  honey
275 g/10 oz self-raising
  flour
grated rind of 1 lemon
demerara sugar to
  sprinkle
Icing
225 g/8 oz icing sugar
1 – 2 tablespoons lemon
  juice
shredded rind of 1 lemon

Serves 6 – 8

Illustrated on the jacket

Place all the ingredients for the cake,
except the demerara sugar, in the bowl.
Mix, using the double-bladed chopping
knife, until smooth.

Turn the cake mixture into a greased
and lined 20-cm/8-inch cake tin, sprinkle
the top with demerara sugar and cook in
a moderate oven (180°C, 350°F, Gas
Mark 4) for 1¼ – 1½ hours. Leave to cool in
the tin, then turn out onto a cake rack.

To make the lemon icing, sieve the
icing sugar into a small mixing bowl.
Add the lemon juice and mix with the
sugar to give a soft, flowing icing. Pour
the icing over the cake, spreading with a
palette knife or spatula. Decorate with
shredded lemon rind.

◙ Muesli

50 g/2 oz dried apricots
50 g/2 oz almonds or
  walnuts
25 g/1 oz dried apple
  rings
1 tablespoon dried milk
  powder
1 tablespoon brown sugar
100 g/4 oz porridge oats
1 tablespoon wheat germ
50 g/2 oz raisins
To serve
milk
a little natural yogurt

Serves 4

Chop the apricots, nuts and apple rings,
using the double-bladed chopping knife.

Mix together the dried milk powder,
sugar, oats, wheat germ and raisins. Stir
in the chopped ingredients. Just before
serving, pour on milk and top with a little
natural yogurt.

Note Larger quantities of the dried
mixture may be made up and stored in
an air-tight container.

preserves

Since the majority of the work in preserving is in the initial preparation, the food processor is an invaluable aid. Vegetables and fruits are chopped shredded or reduced to a purée in seconds. No more watery eyes from chopping onions or stained hands from such vegetables as beetroot either! When jams or marmalades are being made, it is important to ensure that the pan used is large enough to allow for rapid boiling once the sugar has been dissolved. To test for setting point, a sugar thermometer may be used, in which case a temperature of between 104°C/220°F and 107°C/225°F will be reached when the preserve is at setting point. Alternatively, a little of the preserve may be dropped onto a cold saucer. If setting point has been reached, a skin will form over the top as it cools, and it will no longer run freely. Remove the pan from the heat as soon as setting point is reached.

Pickled red cabbage

1 large red cabbage,
   about 1.25 kg/2½ lb
225 g/8 oz salt
2 tablespoons pickling
   spice
1.4 litres/2½ pints white
   vinegar

*Makes about 2 (1-kg/
   2-lb) jars*

Remove the outer leaves from the cabbage and cut the rest into wedges which will fit into the feed tube. Discard the hard core at the base of the cabbage. Shred the cabbage, using the slicing disc, and place alternate layers of this and the salt in a large bowl. Cover and leave overnight.

Place the pickling spice in a saucepan with the vinegar, bring to the boil and simmer for 15 minutes. Cool and strain.

Rinse and dry the cabbage then pack loosely into sterilised jars. Cover the cabbage completely with the cold, spiced vinegar. Allow the cabbage to stand for a week before using. The cabbage will lose its crispness after 2 or 3 months.

Nutty apricot pickle

225 g/8 oz dried
   apricots
450 g/1 lb onions
350 g/12 oz cooking
   apples
225 g/8 oz walnuts
350 g/12 oz brown sugar
juice of 1 large lemon
100 g/4 oz sultanas
300 ml/½ pint vinegar
½ teaspoon salt

*Makes 2.5 – 2.75 kg/
   5½ – 6 lb*

Cover the apricots with water and leave to soak overnight. Peel and quarter the onions and chop roughly, using the double-bladed chopping knife. Place the onion in a large saucepan. Peel, core and quarter the apples and chop roughly, using the double-bladed chopping knife. Add the apple to the onion in the pan. Drain the apricots and chop roughly, using the double-bladed chopping knife. Chop the walnuts in the same way and add to the pan with the apricots, together with all the remaining ingredients.

Bring the mixture to the boil, reduce the heat and simmer for 30 – 40 minutes, until the liquid has evaporated and the pickle is thick. Pour into warmed, sterilised jars and cover while still hot.

✿ Pepper and onion pickle

Illustrated on page 112

Quarter the peppers, remove the seeds and chop roughly, using the double-bladed chopping knife. Peel and quarter the onions, chop roughly in the same way and place in a large saucepan with the chopped peppers. Cut the dates into small pieces and chop, using the double-bladed chopping knife. Add to the peppers and onions together with all the other ingredients. Stir well.

Bring the mixture to the boil then reduce the heat, cover and simmer for $1\frac{1}{2}$–$1\frac{3}{4}$ hours. Pour the pickle into warmed sterilised jars and cover while hot.

4 large green peppers
1 kg/2 lb onions
225 g/8 oz cooking dates
350 g/12 oz granulated
    sugar
300 ml/$\frac{1}{2}$ pint tarragon
    vinegar
1 teaspoon salt

*Makes 1.5-1.75 kg/
    3–4 lb*

✿ Marrow chutney

Cut the marrow into large chunks and chop roughly, using the double-bladed chopping knife. Place layers of the chopped marrow in a large bowl and sprinkle each layer generously with the salt. Cover and leave to stand overnight. Drain the liquid from the marrow, and rinse off the remaining salt. Drain and place in a large saucepan.

Peel and quarter the onions and chop roughly, using the double-bladed chopping knife. Add to the saucepan with the marrow. Peel and core the cooking apples and chop roughly, using the double-bladed chopping knife. Add to the marrow and onion together with the remaining ingredients.

Bring the mixture to the boil then simmer for 45 minutes or until the chutney is soft and thick. Turn into dry, sterilised jars which have been warmed. Cover the chutney while it is still hot.

1 (1.75 kg/4 lb) marrow,
    seeds removed and
    peeled
175 g/6 oz salt
450 g/1 lb onions
450 g/1 lb cooking
    apples
350 g/12 oz soft brown
    sugar
350 g/12 oz sultanas
600 ml/1 pint vinegar

Makes 2.25 kg/5 lb

◨ Beetroot chutney

1 kg/2 lb cooked
   beetroot, peeled
450 g/1 lb onions
450 g/1 lb cooking
   apples
600 ml/1 pint red wine
   vinegar
225 g/8 oz brown sugar
100 g/4 oz sultanas
4 cloves
1 teaspoon salt
¼ teaspoon ground
   ginger

Makes 2.75 kg/6 lb

Illustrated on page 112
Quarter the beetroot and chop roughly, using the double-bladed chopping knife. Place in a large saucepan. Peel and quarter the onions and chop roughly in the same way. Add to the beetroot in the saucepan. Peel, core and quarter the apples and chop roughly, using the double-bladed chopping knife. Mix with the beetroot and onion in the pan.

Add all the remaining ingredients and bring to the boil, stirring all the time. Reduce the heat, cover the pan and simmer for 1 – 1½ hours. Pour into warmed, sterilised jars and cover while still hot.

◨ Mint chutney

1.5 kg/3 lb cooking
   apples
450 g/1 lb onions
300 ml/½ pint white
   vinegar
350 g/12 oz granulated
   sugar
175 g/6 oz mint, left in a
   bowl of water

Makes 2 – 2.25 kg/
4½ – 5 lb

Peel, core and quarter the apples and chop roughly, using the double-bladed chopping knife. Place in a large saucepan. Peel and quarter the onions and chop roughly in the same way. Add the onions to the apples in the saucepan, together with the vinegar and sugar.

Bring the mixture to the boil, reduce the heat and simmer for 45 minutes – 1 hour until it is soft with no excess liquid. Meanwhile, remove the leaves from the washed mint. Dry the mint leaves and chop finely, using the double-bladed chopping knife. Stir the chopped mint into the cooked chutney. Pour into warmed, sterilised jars and cover while hot.

Blackberry relish

Purée the blackberries, using the double-bladed chopping knife and pour into a large saucepan. Peel and quarter the onions, and chop roughly, using the double-bladed chopping knife. Add to the blackberry purée. Remove the seeds from the pepper and cut into chunks. Chop roughly together with the preserved ginger, using the double-bladed chopping knife. Add to the saucepan. Quarter the apples and chop roughly, using the double-bladed chopping knife. Add to the ingredients in the saucepan, together with the brown sugar, vinegar, turmeric and ground cloves. Stir the mixture well.

Bring to the boil, reduce the heat and simmer for 1 – 1½ hours, until the mixture is soft and thick. Stir in the sweet corn. Pour into warmed, sterilised jars and cover while still hot.

1 kg/2 lb blackberries, washed and drained
350 g/12 oz onions
1 large green pepper
3 pieces preserved ginger
350 g/12 oz cooking apples, peeled and cored
225 g/8 oz brown sugar
300 ml/½ pint vinegar
½ teaspoon turmeric
¼ teaspoon ground cloves
1 (198-g/7-oz) can sweet corn, drained

Makes about 1.5 – 1.75 kg/3 – 4 lb

🔒 🔓 Peach conserve

2 lemons
1 cooking apple
1 kg/2 lb ripe peaches
   (about 8 peaches)
175 ml/6 fl oz water
800 g/1¾ lb sugar

Makes 1.5 kg/3 lb

Peel the zest from the lemons, being careful not to include any pith. Chop very finely, using the double-bladed chopping knife and place in a large saucepan. Peel, core and quarter the apple and chop finely, using the double-bladed chopping knife. Add to the lemon zest in the saucepan. Place the peaches in a large bowl, cover with boiling water and leave to stand for a minute. Drain off the water and peel the peaches. Discard the peach stones and pack the peach halves into the feed tube. Slice, using the slicing disc. Add to the saucepan with the water, lemon and apple and bring to the boil. Reduce the heat, cover the saucepan and simmer for about 35–40 minutes or until the fruit is soft.

Add the sugar and stir until dissolved. Bring to the boil and boil rapidly until setting point is reached – about 15–20 minutes (see page 119). Allow the jam to stand for a few minutes, then pour into warmed sterilised jars.

◙ Honeyed lemon marmalade

Illustrated on the jacket

Carefully peel the zest from the lemons. Squeeze out the lemon juice and pour into a large saucepan. Chop the zest, using the double-bladed chopping knife and add to the lemon juice together with the water. Cut what is left of the lemons into quarters and chop roughly, using the double-bladed chopping knife. Place in a muslin bag, tie the opening securely and add to the saucepan with the lemon mixture. Bring to the boil, reduce the heat and simmer for 1½–2 hours until the zest is soft. Remove the muslin bag from the liquid and squeeze any liquid from it.

Add the sugar and honey to the liquid and stir until it has dissolved completely. Bring to the boil and boil rapidly until setting point is reached – about 20 minutes. Remove the pan from the heat immediately setting point is reached (see page 119) and cool slightly until a skin forms on the surface of the marmalade. Stir the marmalade well and pour into warmed, sterilised jars. Cover when cold.

4 large lemons
1.4 litres/2½ pints water
900 g/2 lb sugar
225 g/8 oz honey

Makes 1.5 kg/3 lb

Index